Guvn

Mickey Francis, thirty-seven, was born and raised in Moss Side, Manchester. A football hooligan since his youth, he has numerous convictions for violence-related offences, has served two prison terms and is currently banned from every soccer ground in Britain.

Peter Walsh, thirty-four, is a sub-editor with the *Manchester Evening News*. He previously worked as a reporter for the *Daily Mail*, *The Sun*, and the *Coventry Evening Telegraph*. He is the author of one other book, *Men of Steel: The Lives and Times of Boxing's Middleweight Champions*.

Mickey Francis with Peter Walsh

# Guvnors

Milo Books

Typeset by Intype London Ltd

Printed by Guernsey Press, Channel Islands

MILO BOOKS
PO Box 153, Bury BL0 9FX

To all the football firms that stood and fought on the terraces.

# Contents

# *Prologue*

'FRANCIS. Stand up.'

Judge Denis Clark of the Northern Circuit glowered at me through spectacles the size of welding goggles from his bench in one of the modern, air-conditioned rooms at Liverpool Crown Court. He was not happy.

It was the morning of June 5, 1989. Two months earlier, Judge Clark had listened, frowning, as a Crown prosecutor and police witnesses described a grim catalogue of violence at football grounds across England. He watched secretly-shot video film showing fights and beatings and pitch invasions. He heard how the brutality was organised 'like a military operation' by two gangs of Manchester City supporters known as the Guvnors and the Young Guvnors. And he was told that the kingpin behind it all, the hooligan-in-chief, was me. Michael 'Mickey' Francis.

It had been sixteen long months since my arrest as I lay in bed before dawn at my home in Manchester. In the time since then, I had been locked up in jail on remand and then released on bail, had pleaded not guilty and then changed my plea. My name had appeared in the national Press and on TV, always with the words 'vicious' or 'thug' attached. Now I was facing the last kick of the penalty shoot-out with my hands tied behind my back.

The judge scratched his black beard, adjusted his long white wig, and addressed me in measured tones with a hint of a Scouse accent.

'The consequences of your behaviour are widespread. They tarnish the good name which football has built up for well over 100 years. They damage national pride and they do incalculable damage to our international sporting prestige.'

Fair enough.

'I have a great deal of sympathy with Manchester City. There is nothing they could have done to prevent determined hooliganism. This noble and famous club is to be in no way besmirched or tarnished by your behaviour.'

Noble and famous? They're crap.

'The common denominator is the thrill of violence . . .'

Now you're talking. It is a thrill. It's a fucking buzz like nothing else. To stand there with your lads on a strange street in a strange town, confronted by a baying, half-pissed mob raging in a frenzy because you have dared to come on *their* manor, outnumbered, facing bricks and sticks and bottles and bats and knives and God knows what else – and to have it. To stand and take them on and never run.

'The general public are sick to the back teeth of such Saturday afternoon, indiscriminate, recreational, part-time violence . . .'

That's a good phrase. Recreational violence. For me and thousands like me, from Carlisle to Plymouth, from Newcastle to Brighton. Young men who share the same wicked passion, derive the same satisfaction when they walk through the streets en masse and watch the passers-by stare in shock and horror and feel the same heart-pumping adrenalin surge when they steam into another gang in a roaring, kicking, punching frenzy. It's what we do.

Judge Clark went on and on. My family looked ashen in the public gallery. It was harder for them than it was for me. Reporters sat with pens scribbling on the Press bench, preserving the judge's words for posterity. I felt sick in the pit of my stomach. I was going to get slammed here, five years at least, maybe seven. Seven years in a shithole like Strangeways, with junkies and idiots for company. Just say it, say what you have to say. Then I'll know where I stand. I can do the time. Just tell me.

And then he paused, took a quick, direct look at me, and said, 'I sentence you to . . .

*  *  *

When I was sent to jail at the age of twenty-nine, I had spent precisely half of my life in the pursuit of football violence. From 1974 to 1988, it dominated my thoughts and filled my spare time; at first, the fighting, but later the planning, organisation, travelling and socialising as well. With my brothers, Donald and Chris, I was eventually instrumental in the instigation of thuggery on a grand scale. I rose from young fringe member to 'top boy,' one of perhaps a couple of hundred men across the country who led their troops into combat every Saturday in the towns and cities of Britain.

I have had hundreds of fights, on the terraces and in shopping centres, in pubs and night clubs, in motorway cafes and train stations. I have been stabbed, hit with iron bars and beer glasses, kicked unconscious, punched and butted. I have been threatened with death by people who meant it. I have been chased alone through dark alleys, hunted like a dog, and suffered cracked ribs and broken hands and black eyes and bloody noses. I have dodged bricks, coins, rocks, cans, distress flares, planks of wood and bottles filled with piss. I have been beaten by policemen, arrested, fined and thrown in jail. And I have dished it out. In spades.

This is the story of my life: a journey into the dark side of our national game. It contains some nasty episodes. Many people will find it horrifying. Others may be disgusted. Well, I'm not sorry. I make no apologies because I don't regret what I did. I fought with those who wanted to fight with me. I didn't beat up parents with their children. I didn't batter little old ladies. The people you will read about on these pages, the ones I attacked and who attacked me, were as up for it as I was. They *loved* it. And few of them were badly hurt. A football fight looks ten times worse than it really is. Keeping your nerve is the important thing.

I was attracted to football as a sport like every other kid in my area; I took to thuggery because that's the person I was. My brothers were the same. Donald, the oldest, was a charismatic figure who organised one of the premier gangs of the 1970s, the so-called Cool Cats. They were unknown to the media but fellow hooligans learned to respect and fear them. Later, as I will describe, the clique changed in character and personnel and adopted the name of the Mayne Line Service Crew, making newspaper headlines around the country. Finally it changed again, to the Guvnors, the crew which I was jailed for leading, a hard-core firm of experienced battlers taking one last plunge on the terrace rollercoaster. Those three gangs spanned the heyday of the worst – or best – years of the hooligan culture, from the crazy boot-boy days of the mid-seventies to the 'casual' gangs and the ground-wrecking sprees of the eighties. There is nothing like them now at Manchester City, and for that many people will breath a sigh of relief.

I have tried to set down events as accurately as I can and to check dates wherever possible. But anyone who has ever had a fight will tell you that time bends, your vision plays tricks and your thinking distorts. Ten people involved in the same scrap will tell ten different stories of what happened. It's not always easy to assess how many people were involved in a particular incident and the exact order of events. I have tried my best to be honest and fair. If you were there, and you remember it differently, too bad. Write your own book.

Some names have been changed and some left out. Those of my mates whose names appear in this book have generally been before the courts and paid for what they did and, like me, no longer participate. Unlike many hooligans, I can talk about my role because I have taken my medicine and served my time. Others are still active and must remain anonymous. If anyone is named here who didn't want to be, then I'm sorry, but it would have taken years to track down everyone to ask their permission. You're an elusive bunch at the best of times.

Quite a few books have been written about hooliganism. I have read some of them. This one is different, I believe, in that it is the first by someone who was actively involved in the leadership of an English soccer gang, someone who was centre stage. A Scottish lad wrote something similar a few years ago about Aberdeen. It was quite good but, with respect, this is England, mate. Different ball game.

Unlike some, I don't seek to justify what I did. I wasn't fighting for my country's honour or defending my home. I was a thug, pure and simple. Nor am I one of those figures beloved of the media, the 'successful professional' or City yuppie who lives in a suburb and wears his hooligan credentials like a fashion accessory. I was born and raised in a slum in one of the toughest inner-city areas in Europe, a district that saw some of the worst urban riots of this century. I have been in trouble with the law almost continuously from childhood. If I hadn't become a football hooligan, what would I have been? Rich or dead, I would say.

Finally, this is not a sociological analysis of soccer thuggery. That doesn't interest me. You won't find any musings on the state of the nation, the plight of the underclass or the ethics of pro-active policing. This book is an attempt to tell people what happened, how it really was for those of us who spent our mid-week nights and Saturday afternoons roaming in search of violence.

# 1

## Moss Side

A CAR pulls up in a dark, deserted street. The driver is an overweight white man in his early fifties in a business suit, shirt and tie. His passenger is a black girl in her late teens, wearing too much make up and too few clothes. The man is her first client of the night. They talk briefly, then climb into the back seat. The girl removes her knickers and hitches up her leather mini skirt. She starts to unzip the man's trousers.

A few yards yards away, in a derelict house that borders a small park, a figure moves in the shadows. It is joined by another, then another, until twenty phantoms emerge from the shell of the building. Silently they surround the car.

The fat man is on top of the woman now, oblivious. His trousers are at his ankles and his pale bare backside is moving up and down, faster and faster. He is lost in lust. Then the whore looks over his shoulder and her face freezes. She swears and pulls away. The man jerks his head, blinking, to see twenty ragamuffin youths, their faces half-hidden by scarves, staring menacingly into the car. A stocky, school-age urchin with coffee skin and afro hair yanks open the door.

'Give us your fucking money.'

The man pulls frantically at his trousers but a dozen hands are already in the car, raking pockets, snatching a bag, tugging at his gold wristwatch. The prostitute kicks out but the man is too terrified to fight back. Then the children are gone, as quickly as they came, back into the crumbling houses with a wallet stuffed with cash and a watch and a handbag, the price for entering the streets that my brothers and I considered our own.

Welcome to Moss Side.

\* \* \*

Manchester City are in my blood. I was born five minutes' walk from the the ground, in the front room of a small terraced house in Acomb Street, in the heart of the old Moss Side slums. Step out of our front door and look to the right and you could see the Maine Road floodlights over the rooftops. On match days the streets would fill up with cars and people and you could hear every roar and chant from the terraces and smell the burgers and hot dogs from the stalls outside.

Moss Side later became infamous for guns, gangs and drugs. But in the late 1950s, before the land clearances and the building of the mid- and high-rise blocks in Hulme, it was a typical old-fashioned northern community, poor but friendly. The houses were built in neat rows, with back yards and cobbled alleys and ginnels and a shop or a pub on nearly every corner. The television series *Coronation Street* is based on Salford, across the city, but it could just as easily have been Acomb Street.

My dad, Ezra Francis, was born in Saint Catherine, Jamaica, one of eleven children. They were ruled with the rod by their parents. Ezra was a good runner and boxer at school and needed to be; Jamaica was a rough place. The men would drink in rum bars, like pubs, and would often challenge each other to fights. They would go outside and clash with sticks in a certain style, like a martial art. Afterwards, winner and loser would return to the bar and have a drink together. My dad later told me, 'I used to watch them as a child and want to be like them. It was bred into you. A lot of Jamaicans like to fight.'

He made the three-week boat journey to England when he was twenty-three, looking for work. The usual destinations for Caribbean people were Moss Side, Toxteth in Liverpool, Handsworth in Birmingham, Notting Hill or Brixton in London. My dad stayed with an aunt in Manchester and found a job within a week as a welder, first among the heavy industries of Trafford Park and later at Stockport. By then he was a strapping bloke, only five feet nine inches tall but fourteen stone of solid muscle. He trained at a local gym, body-building, and soon became a feared streetfighter in the Moss Side area. He wouldn't let anyone insult his fellow countrymen. At weekends he sometimes went with friends to night clubs in the city and fought the white Teddy Boy gangs. The black lads would gather on one side of a club and the Teds on the other, in their zoot suits, and sooner or later it would erupt. Usually the black lads had to scarper because they were heavily out-numbered. My dad thought it was all a bit of harmless fun, unlike today, when you can wind up dead if you upset the wrong guy.

One of the clubs was called the Palm Beach and it was there that he met my mum, a Scouser called Dorothy Hughes. Her family came originally from Wales but she was born in the Dingle and raised in Toxteth, two of the toughest areas of Liverpool. Her dad was a 'checker' on the docks, checking cargoes in and out. She moved to Moss Side when she was twenty and met my dad within

3

a few weeks. The fact that she was white and he was black caused a few problems with her family; mixed marriages were frowned on then. But it made no difference to my parents and eventually they moved in together. In 1959 they had a son, Donald, and found a house in Acomb Street, a small road with Manchester University at one end and Whitworth Park at the other. The house had three bedrooms and two rooms downstairs. The front room was let to lodgers and the middle room was for entertaining dad's friends. There was a kitchen at the back and a cellar. Dad's pals were mainly West Indian and they had parties all the time, crowding in for a gamble and a drink. It wasn't exactly a shebeen but it wasn't far off.

I arrived a year after Donald, on April 11, 1960. I was born in the front room, while my dad went out the back to do some painting. Finally came our Chris in 1962 to complete the trio. Like my dad, my mam worked hard, as a cleaner at Ducie High School, just across the road, in the mornings and at Manchester Royal Infirmary, the city's main hospital, in the afternoons. She has always been a most loving mother and given one hundred per cent to her children but it was a struggle to make ends meet. She would leave the house at 5am, come back at 8.30am to get us to school, then work again until the early evening. As I got older it was my job to make the tea for my brothers while she was out. My cooking skills never extended further than sausages, beans and instant mash but then we had no money for anything fancy. However, mam made sure we always got presents at Christmas and birthdays and she made great occasions of things like Hallowe'en.

My dad started to take body-building seriously and

won the Mister Manchester title and Mister North West Britain in 1962. He travelled all over to holiday resorts like Blackpool, Morecambe and the Isle of Man, posing in what were then called physique shows. One day someone suggested he try wrestling. He did, and came home with a cauliflower ear, but enjoyed it and was soon appearing in professional shows at places like the Free Trade Hall and eventually on TV with the likes of Earl Maynard, Paul Winter, Mick McManus, Jackie Pallo and Jack Cassidy, who was very dirty and used to spit water in his opponents' faces. Dad fought under the name Sugar Ray Dodo; his best mate was called Honey Boy Zimba. They trained at the Sunfist Gym in Levenshulme and at Ardwick Lads' Club, where the sessions were run by a guy called the Black Panther.

I loved my childhood and, looking back, I wouldn't change a thing. But what I remember most was the violence. My dad was violent to his sons and we were violent to each other. With the wrestling on top of the long hours he worked as a welder, sometimes he wouldn't come home for days, but when he did, he was brutal. He was very strict and we were beaten for the slightest thing. If something was damaged or went missing in the house, he wouldn't ask who was responsible; he would beat all of us. He would assemble us in the room and close the door. Then he would take off his belt, hold both your hands in one of his, and belt fuck out of you. He was so strong that there was nothing you could do to get away. He always did Donald first because he was the oldest. Donald would yell and me and Chris would start screaming before we had even been hit.

Sometimes he would make me stand on one leg in a

corner with my hands on my head. On Sundays we had to clean a room each in the house for him to inspect. If we failed the inspection, off came his belt. He whacked us so hard that we would have blood blisters on our arms and legs. It became so bad that when he walked into the living room, we would all walk out. We just didn't want to be in his way. It was like, 'Dad's here, let's go.'

When I was about fifteen, I took £6 in coppers from his change jar. He had been in a car crash shortly before and was using a walking stick. He demanded to know who had taken the money and Donald said it was me. I thought he wouldn't be able to do anything because of his injury, but he pinned me against the wall with one hand and beat seven bells out of me with the stick. I couldn't walk for two days.

One day Donald challenged him and said, 'Why don't you treat me like a man?'

Dad said, 'Okay, I will.'

And he punched Donald on the jaw and knocked him out.

My mam used to stay out of the way. There was nothing she could do. Then one night he had a go at her. The three of us went upstairs, got a poker and threatened him with it. For once, that made him stop.

I still love my dad and now he's one of my best friends, but I wouldn't bring up my kids that way. As an adult I believe in a tooth for a tooth, an eye for an eye, but what he did to us was too much. I think he did it because he was raised that way himself. It may also have been why my brothers and I became so violent. In our childhood, if we did anything wrong, we got battered. So if someone did something to me, real or imagined, my first instinct was to hit out.

Fortunately, most of the time my dad wasn't around. We would get up to all sorts of mischief. The three of us had the most horrendous fights. My dad wanted us to be able to look after ourselves and taught us boxing and wrestling moves when we were very young. We developed little territories. Chris and I shared a bed while Donald had his own room. Donald is one of the hardest guys I have ever known and you couldn't step on to his carpet without getting weighed in.

We were all as bad as each other. During the power cuts in the mid-seventies, we would sit in front of the coal fire toasting bread on forks. We would argue over this toast all night. On one occasion, Donald and Chris started fighting. Chris grabbed the toast and made a break for it, slamming the glass panel door that separated the downstairs rooms. The door shut so hard on Donald's hand that it cut off the end of a finger. Chris stood on the finger tip in his bare feet, picked it up and threw it on the fire.

Another time, Chris was having a bath. I walked into the bathroom just as he was leaning over to turn the tap off. It was too good an opportunity to miss; I grabbed a toothbrush off the shelf and stuck it up his arse. He went mad. Later that night, to get his own back, he sneaked across the room while I was lying in bed and pissed all over me.

Now, to a lot of people, that might not seem like normal behaviour but in our house it was going on all the time. My mum is only little and she was helpless. Our fights would scare her witless and she would go into spasms to make us stop. Sometimes she would take her slipper off and beat us but it never hurt. We'd pretend to cry, go upstairs and laugh about it. The payback came when my old man returned from work. He'd walk in and murder us.

Despite the hidings, I loved my life as a kid. It was an adventure. We lived in the re-development area. Whole streets of slums were being pulled down. Everywhere were empty houses, bulldozers, bricks to throw, windows to smash. What more could you want as a kid? We could do as much damage as we wanted; it didn't matter, because everything was coming down anyway. Bonfire Nights were fantastic because we had so much to burn. It was a giant adventure playground and in our area there were loads of kids. I grew up with big Irish families like the Ryans and the Kellys. Many of them still live in the area. Anything that went wrong was always down to either the Francis brothers or the Ryans. They were a good family: Tommy, Ged, Terence, a load of them. Then there was Vernon, Tony and Trevor Dore, the Hewitts, all good lads. We were always out. You'd get out of bed in the morning and go and sit on the wall and you'd be out, have your breakfast and you'd be out, your tea and you'd be out.

We played all the street games, valley-vo one-two-three, British bulldogs. We organised raids and ambushes in the derelict houses, splitting into groups, ten kids inside the house and twenty outside. The ones outside had to break in while the ones inside put up barricades to stop them. If you got caught you were tortured. That was how we developed little gangs, from the age of ten or eleven. Each patch of streets had its own 'firm'. We were from Acomb Street and Cecil Street and we stuck together, twenty or thirty young lads, all on racing bikes. We nicked bikes from the students at the university next door. We called their security staff the 'Green Men' because they wore green overalls. You knew it was time to leg it when you heard someone shout, 'The Green Men are coming.'

My mam nearly killed Donald when she found out that all the big flashy lights on his bike had been stolen. We were hanging about in the park one evening when she marched up with an axe. She said to Donald, 'Where did you get those fucking lights from?'

Before he could think of some tale, she hacked the bike to bits in front of all his mates. He was devastated.

It was my mum who made Donald have his first street-fight, the first of hundreds. John Ryan had kicked him and our Chris in a row and Donald went in bleating to my mum. Now my mum is very staunch. No matter what we did, she was with us all the way; we were always her babies. But she said to Donald, 'If you don't go back out there and stick up for yourself, I'll leather you.'

So Donald had to go out and fight John and ended up battering him.

None of us was a big success at school. We went to the old Webster Street Junior School, now Moss Side police station. The playground was on the roof, with a wall around it. Donald was always getting sent up there for misbehaving during lessons, while Chris once threw a chair at a teacher. I had my first fight there when I was ten. It was over a duffel coat. This kid was wearing it and for some reason I wanted it and swore blind it was mine. I grabbed him by the hood of his coat and swung him round by his neck. We started fighting. Somebody else joined in and I got a kicking, lost my first fight.

Donald went to Central Saviour secondary school in Kirkmanshulme Lane while Chris and I went to Nichols Ardwick High School, now Ellen Wilkinson High, on Hyde Road. The nearest school to us was Ducie High, just across the road, but mam didn't want me to go there because all the other neighbourhood kids were there and she wanted to keep us away from the riff-raff, as she called them, not knowing I was riff-raff. So she sent us to Ardwick.

It was a good school and I enjoyed my first year. Some of the teachers used to call me 'coffee-coloured boy' because of the colour of my skin. But when I reached thirteen and started noticing girls and other distractions, I lost interest in education. I became a teacher's nightmare. I wouldn't concentrate or do as I was told. I wasn't a rebel, because I believe in discipline and authority, but I was too easily distracted. I wanted to be the centre of attention and I was hyperactive. Even today I don't sleep much. We had the cane, the slipper and the strap and they must have been sick of strapping my hand. I couldn't keep out of trouble.

I went out one dinner time and asked a lad for a chip. He wouldn't give me one, so I pinched his watch. That night my mum said, 'Where did you get that watch?'

'This lad lent it me for the night, mam.'

I think she would have believed me if the police hadn't knocked on our door shortly afterwards. 'I was going to give it back tomorrow, mam,' I said.

I got in more bother when the school took us to an outdoor pursuit centre in the Lake District. We had been there only a few hours and were playing football. I kicked the ball and it hit a lad in the bollocks. It must have hurt but he played up on it and I got a bit of mither off the teachers. I was fuming, so I beat up the lad for getting me in trouble. This big gym teacher called Mr Maloney, who hated my guts, went nuts. He put me in his car and drove me straight back to Manchester.

I had loads of fights. I started boxing at a club after school and thought I was Jack the Lad in the playground. I battered everyone; I never had much of a challenge because most of the others were there to learn while I was boisterous and out of control. Of the three of us, Donald is the most intelligent, but I don't think any of us took any exams. I'm not stupid, I can put myself across, read and write, but general knowledge is not my thing. Chris was the same. He went wild at school. The pair of us stuck together. Even today, he's my closest friend. We've always had a bond; even when we were sent to prison, we went together. I can't do fuck all on my own!

Finally, when I was fourteen, I attacked a teacher, had a complete tantrum and pretty much wrecked a classroom. They threw me out. I walked across the field outside the school giving the V-sign and shouting 'fuck off' to the headmaster.

'Don't come back, Francis,' he shouted back.

So I was kicked out of school with no qualifications. No other school would take me. I was off suspended for almost a year. Then I went back for about four months. My mam said to me, 'Just try and stay to sort yourself out.'

The teachers, who couldn't wait to see the back of me, said, 'We have found a job for you if you want it, at the Co-op.'

It was for £24 a week, packing flour. I took it and left school at fifteen. My expulsion hadn't improved my behaviour in the slightest, however. Our fights at home became so bad that on occasions mam had to call the police. Once, when I was at the Co-op, I left some money at home and it disappeared. I accused Chris of taking it and we started fighting in the bedroom. Donald came in and attacked me for picking on Chris, so the pair of us turned on Donald. That was the sort of bond I had with Chris, although he and I have had our moments. One time, we were in the back yard, building a dog kennel. I was fixing the roof and Chris was down below. I thought, I'd love to drop a brick on his head.

'Chris, the wind's blowing the bricks off.'

'Fuck off, there's no wind.'

So I threw a brick at the back of his head. It was a bit harder than I intended. He ended up with thirty-two stitches.

By this time I had a girlfriend but was spending most evenings down at the boxing gym. One night I cycled home and saw this couple on the floor through our living room window. I peered a bit closer and saw Chris snogging with my girlfriend. I ran in the house, he ran up the stairs and she ran out. I got my own back some time later. Chris was seeing a girl called Maureen from Fallowfield but was sent to borstal for something or other. While he was away I began seeing her without telling him. When he came out, he went out with her again, until one night he walked her to catch her bus home. Standing at the bus stop chatting, he saw some graffiti out of the corner of his eye: 'Mike and Mo.' That's when he tumbled. He wasn't pleased.

Sex wasn't exactly a secret round our way. We never encountered drugs when we were growing up, despite Moss Side's current reputation, but there was a lot of prostitution, and still is. That's how we came to organise our little team to rob the tarts and their customers. They would pick up punters in Whalley Range and other places and get them to drive down to Cecil Street, which was being demolished and was nice and secluded, to do the business. We'd hide in the houses or behind walls, let them get going, then blitz them. We'd surround the car, take the piss out of them, terrify them, pull open the doors, rob everything we could get our hands on and sometimes smash the car up as well. They couldn't exactly go to the police.

One time there was a bloke and a girl in a van. He was getting his end away and we pulled open the doors to rob them. One of the lads called Tony jumped into the front of the van and the bloke pulled the door shut and tried to drive off with Tony inside. By the time he managed to scramble out, he had nearly turned white. We were killing ourselves.

Donald emerged as the leader of our group. He and Vernon Dore, who was also very handy, used to fight each other every summer, taking their shirts off and going to it in the park, a kind of annual contest to see who was the hardest. The mums used to come out screaming, dragging them apart. Donald's similar in build to me, not tall but stocky. When it comes to the crunch, he's one hundred per cent loyal and as game as they come, as many a victim can testify. But I have to say he's off his head. He's obsessed with tidiness and if you went into his room or touched his stuff he would kick off. He used to come in and weigh us in. As we got a bit older, me and Chris thought, we'll fucking have him one day. In the end the pair of us did him, out in the street. It took two of us though.

My dad first took me to the Sunfist Gym when I was eleven. I did a bit of weight training, then moved to the Cavendish Boxing Club in Hulme. I was pretty good in the gym but when it came to boxing in front of an audience I seemed to develop stage fright and never did myself justice. I had a few amateur fights, won a few, lost a few, nothing fantastic. Through the boxing I also started to meet and mix with lads from other areas like Hulme and Stretford. We were developing a close-knit group and if we went somewhere we went in numbers. If you're in numbers, you're strong. If we went to Hulme we'd go twenty-handed. If we went to Stretford, we'd go the same. You wouldn't go on your own, or in twos and three, because somewhere along the line one of us would have done something to upset someone there. We all had cliques. We'd burn each others bonfires down, that sort of stuff.

There were no rival gangs within Moss Side itself, like the ones that developed later. You were all together. Things have changed; it's not nice any more. My dad still lives in the same house in Acomb Street but he's always moaning about Moss Side going downhill, with the drugs and street crime, old ladies scared to go out of their houses. But he'll never move. He still works out at the gym and drives a taxi now. Unfortunately he and my mum are separated. After thirty-odd years she walked out. I think she'd had enough of the family problems and her sons getting into trouble.

My dad always says, 'I walk behind the law, not in front of the law.' That's the way he wanted us to be and fear of my dad kept some sort of check on us. Then one day when I was in my mid-teens, a telegram arrived from Jamaica. My grandfather had died. Dad travelled

over there to entomb him, which is a tradition in the
West Indies, and was gone for six weeks. With him away,
we went berserk. Donald immediately got in trouble with
the police and Chris and I soon followed. It was one
thing after another. That was when we really went off
the rails.

# 2
## *Junior Blue*

FRANCIS Lee, Colin Bell, Mike Summerbee, Tony Book, Joe Corrigan . . . the names roll off the tongue of anyone who supported Manchester City in the glory days of the late 1960s. City then had one of the most successful teams in British football, under the great manager-coach partnership of Joe Mercer and Malcolm Allison. In 1966, we were promoted as champions of the old Second Division. Two years later, when I was seven, the Blues won the League title for only the second time in their history, before an average home crowd of more than 37,000. In 1969, we beat Leicester City 1–0 at Wembley to win the FA Cup and in 1970 brought home the European Cup Winners' Cup and the League Cup. Four major honours in three seasons: unimaginable now.

To us kids from Moss Side, City were magic. We would run across Whitworth Park to see the team parading down Oxford Road in an open-topped bus, holding up their latest piece of silverware on the way to yet another rapturous reception in Albert Square. Youngsters want to follow a winning team – they're all wearing Man United shirts these days – and I was no exception.

I saw my first game at the age of five, perched on my dad's shoulders in what is now the North Stand. My dad is City mad; he's had a season ticket for nearly thirty years and still attends every home match. He took me and Donald as soon as we were old enough, lifting us over the turnstiles; in those days you didn't pay for young kids, not if you knew the gatemen. We were too little to take much interest in the game. Instead we would run around through the legs of the adults, playing ticky-it, or tag, occasionally cheering and jumping about when there was a goal, until it was time to go home.

As we got older and more independent, we wanted to go with our mates rather than my dad. We were always self-reliant. The problem was, we never had any money. Quite a lot from our area supported United but they rarely went to Old Trafford because to go there you had to get the bus and to get the bus you had to have money. Sometimes we would try to jib in over the wall or the turnstiles. It was only when we started minding cars that we earned enough to pay in.

Any fan who has visited an inner-city ground like Maine Road or Anfield will be familiar with the little scallies who come up when you've parked before a game and ask, 'Can I mind your car, mister?'

If you say 'no' you spend the whole game worrying about whether the little bastards have run a coin down the side of your prized Ford Escort. We soon clocked on to this as a way of making a few bob and became the unofficial car park attendants for the Acomb Street-Great Western Street area. Any rivals who tried to move in were quickly done over and our first money-making scheme was up and running.

The cannier blokes would offer to pay you after the game, so you wouldn't take the money and disappear, but a lot would bung you some change just to stop you mithering. You got some stroppy cunts but they often came back to find their tyres knifed or let down with a matchstick in the valve. We'd collect as much as we could, leave at five to three to watch the game, then duck out at three-quarter time to be back for those that hadn't paid. I got back a few times and a car we were supposed to be minding had been nicked. We disappeared sharpish. It was rare that anyone came after us and though the police knew what we were doing, they didn't care. We were only kids.

Our first experience of football violence came from minding the cars. West Ham United played at Maine Road in the early 1970s and there was trouble after the game. Blokes were fighting all around the ground and it spilled into the side streets where we were hanging about. West Ham's fans were charging around smashing windows and all the other kids legged it but we stood there with the City men. We didn't actually do much but our mates were impressed, saying, 'Did you see the Francis brothers?'

Gradually I got more into the football scene. City were still going well in the mid-seventies. In 1974, they reached the League Cup final again, losing to Wolves. Two years later, they won the same competition by beating Newcastle 2–1. Denis Tueart scored with an overhead kick. I went down to Wembley with my dad and had a great day. It's still the only thing I've ever seen them win, apart from promotion. In 1977, we finished runners-up in the League but by then I was more interested in what was happening off the pitch. The cash from minding cars meant I could go regularly with my mates, rather than my dad, and that meant I could run amok.

At that time, City were not recognised as having a hard firm. The club was proud of its family image and its Junior Blues scheme, which encouraged youngsters to go to games in a happy, peaceful atmosphere. Fuck that. To me, they were all nobs. My simple view was that if you didn't want to fight for your team, you weren't a City fan. Daft, I know, but there you go. As far as I was concerned, I was City through and through and if you said anything against the team or against the lads, I'd take it all the way.

Maine Road had the potential to be a hotbed of violence. Crowds were huge, segregation crap, policing a joke. Away fans could easily get lost wandering around the narrow streets and dead ends, especially at night. We knew every nook and cranny, where to hide, where to wait, how to get away. Visitors were routinely escorted by the Old Bill but there were dozens of places to launch ambushes without being sussed. The police tended just to react after fights had already started, they weren't good at preventing trouble. You could do almost anything and get away with it.

We started to go on the Kippax, the big section of terracing that ran the length of one side of the ground. This was our 'end,' where all the lads and singers went, and was a target for rival firms. The object of football hooliganism in the mid-seventies was to take the other team's end, be it the Kop at Liverpool, the Stretford End at United, the Shed at Chelsea, the Shelf at Spurs, or wherever. The idea was to arrive mob-handed, infiltrate your opponent's main section and try to take it over. Someone would kick off, fists and feet would fly into the panicking home supporters, the police would charge in and eventually the away firm would either be chucked out or led on to the edge of the pitch and escorted round to their proper section, to the cheers of the away end. The police rarely asked where you were from when you were entering a ground and there was no fencing to keep you apart inside. Even at City–United derbies, fans were separated only by a length of rope.

Stealing scarves was popular with the younger hooligans. Everyone wore scarves, often tied around wrists or hanging from belts. The idea was to collect as many as you could. Usually there wasn't much violence involved; you went up to someone, ripped their scarf off and ran away with it and that was your day made. You'd go to school the next Monday and display your trophy and you were the big hero. My bedroom wall was covered in scarves; my aim was to get one from every club in the First Division. I had loads of Leeds scarves.

The fashion for teenagers then was two-tone pants and brogues and patch pockets, like clowns. The seventies must have had the worst sense of dress ever. All the white lads had long hair while black lads went for massive afros, which didn't do much for you, if you're looking at it now. Match day was something out of a mad film, with the scarves everywhere, the flares, the hair, big rosettes, all your war clothes on. Today the boys might just wear a little lapel badge to show their allegiance but this was well before all the designer gear became fashionable, although I have to admit that the Cockneys even then were smarter than the Manchester lads. You could tell them apart. We never had much money for clobber but my mam would always shell out if we wanted something that everyone else was wearing. We were proper northerners (although I can honestly say I never wore a donkey jacket).

The look changed in the mid-seventies to white butcher's coats or Crombies, skinhead crops, drainpipe jeans worn at half-mast and baseball boots or Dr

Martens. The uniform would still be embellished with scarves and rosettes. I thought it was cool but my dad hated it. He regarded anyone dressed like that as a thug, which wasn't far wrong, and he kept battering me because my turn-ups were getting shorter and shorter. I would take my Doc Marten's to a mate's house and put them on there to go to the match, so my dad wouldn't see me.

My mum had an idea of what we were up to:

The first time I realised they were getting in trouble, there was a beat copper in the area, a real old-timer, and he came to our house and said, 'I've just taken this off your Donald. I took it off him before anything happened.' He handed me a penknife.

Then they would come in talking. In Liverpool we used to chat in backslang and the boys came in one day, obviously having been in some mischief, and started talking in the slang. They didn't realise I understood it and they were talking about fighting. I laughed at them and they said, 'What are you laughing at?'

I said, 'I know what you're saying.'

Ezra used to go mad because he couldn't understand the backslang and they'd use it in front him. Eventually we started to learn about things they had been up to. They would come in with their coats ripped and say some lads had grabbed them, when they had actually been slashed at with Stanley knives.

All the kids round our way learned backslang, a way of jumbling up words that is incomprehensible to anyone who doesn't know it. You could talk in front of outsiders or the police and they wouldn't understand, which was just as well, because soon a lot of the cops at Maine Road knew me by name. I was seen in the area as a rum lad and if there was trouble, I was usually around. On match days they'd single me or Donald out and sometimes they'd say, 'Hey Francis, fuck off. We know your game.' If we were with a little firm they'd chase us off. I gave them loads of lip. I got a few hidings off the police but they would leave it at that, which was all right by me. Anything is better than a charge sheet, something I learned the hard way.

My first arrest was for stealing a car in Moss Side. People rarely locked their car doors in those days and five of us piled into this crappy two-door parked in a side street. My mate Vernon Dore claimed he could drive. I found a scarf, a flat cap and a pair of shades in the glove compartment and put them on and we drove around the streets. It wasn't long before a police car was following us.

Vernon said, 'I'm not fucking stopping.'

'Don't stop then.'

He put his foot down and we had a chase through Ardwick and Moss Side and back again. Today we'd have been caught straight away but police cars then were like Morris Minors and Minis. Eventually we dumped the car in Ardwick and ran off. I climbed on to a roof and lay there, not making a sound. After half an hour, I decided I must be safe, climbed down and started back towards Moss Side. I was so cocky that I was still wearing the hat and scarf.

A police van drove past me. I heard a sudden screech of tyres; it had done a U-turn and was coming for me.

I tried to get through a fence into a park but the copper jumped out and grabbed me.

'I'm arresting you for taking a vehicle without consent, you little bugger.'

He took me to Whitworth Street police station. Vernon was in there as well.

'Say I wasn't there, Mickey,' he whispered, when we were sitting next to each other on a bench.

The cops phoned my mum. She stormed down to the station and marched in as the arresting officer was talking to me. Crack! She slapped me a right-hander across the face, dead hard.

'You little bastard. Is this the sort of life you want?'

I was devastated. The coppers were nearly bursting, trying not to laugh. They thought I was going to get a worse dose at home than I would off them, so they let me go. Outside, I was crying like a kid.

'I'm sorry mam. Why did you hit me?'

'Don't worry about them bastards in there,' she said. 'I had to show them I was a good parent. Now come on and I'll buy you a Kentucky, love.'

She put her arm round me, walked me down to Oxford Road and bought me a big Kentucky meal.

I was in trouble soon after for riding on the back of a motorbike while under-age with one of the Ryans, and copped a fine. My next arrest was a bit more serious. I hit a copper. It wasn't really my fault. I was with the Ryans again and they persuaded my mum to let me go to the Carousel Club in Moss Side at about eleven o'clock one night. We decided to have a race, them going one way and me another. On the way they came across a crate of bottles and chucked a few of them. A policeman, who must have been on a stakeout nearby and was dressed in scruffy civilian clothes, collared them.

I came round the corner to see what appeared to be a tramp hitting my mates. So I ran over and punched him. He shouted out that he was a policeman and grabbed me. More police came from nowhere, there was a struggle and I ended up with a broken nose. I was a mess. They booked me at the station and took me home, where one of them told my dad to get me to hospital. He was so pissed off that he refused. I was back in court and got another fine, although I think the officer who arrested me felt guilty. He realised I was just protecting my mates. I've seen him out in pubs a few times over the years and he always buys me a drink.

★ ★ ★

My first away trip with City was a friendly against Wigan Athletic. I was about fifteen. A little mob of us decided to go because it wasn't too far away. Wigan is a tough little town, very big on rugby league, about twenty miles north-west of Manchester. We'd never been anywhere before and to us it might as well have been on the moon. We got to the town centre by bus, fifteen-handed. There were loads of City about. I didn't know any of the top boys. We just thought we were hard as fuck. We had a drink, got to the ground, watched City win and left.

Then everything erupted. There were fights breaking out and people running everywhere, some to get away, some to join in. Anyone who fell was kicked. It was frightening, but I began to get the buzz. We knew that if we got separated we could get battered, so we stuck tight together, running through the streets, chasing the Wigan, throwing the odd punch or kick. We got to the bus station and had another skirmish, a few punches, no-one badly hurt. A copper grabbed me and gave me a slap. I managed to pull away and disappeared into the crowd, made it to the bus and we were on our way home, all talking at once, swopping war stories.

'Did you see me smack that bloke?'

'Shit, I thought you'd been nicked for certain.'

'Anyone get hurt?'

'We fucking killed them.'

'Next time we'll take loads and really do them.'

In those days, most football fights were scuffles. You never thought to take a knife or to really hurt someone; there might be a few bricks thrown, a bit of a barney and that was it. I wanted more. It appealed to me. When I am in company, I tend to be a bit flamboyant; I'll do anything for a laugh. I didn't notice it until I was older but I suppose football was the outlet for that side of my personality. I realised after the Wigan game just how much I enjoyed that buzz.

I was earning enough money now to start following the team. My Co-op job was decent pay at the time. I was able to give my mam her keep and bought a Carousel 50cc moped. All the boys had bikes, little Suzukis and Hondas. But the work was crap. You even had to put your hand up to go for a piss. I hadn't been there long when the woman in charge said, 'Mike, can you do the bins today?'

I thought, fucking bins, I'm not emptying them. So I threw them all over the floor and walked out. I guess I just don't like being told what to do.

I was on the dole for a bit before starting a window cleaning round with a mate of mine called Ronnie. We were pulling in about £60 a week but we fell out because

Ronnie didn't want to do upstairs windows. He said he was scared of heights. After that I had various jobs. Everything was illegit, so you didn't have to tell the dole about it – a bit of painting and decorating, a bit of this and that.

Any money I made was spent on football. The scene was getting more organised, more tribal, and it wasn't long before I was involved in my first major battle at a home match. Most younger, would-be hooligans start off on the fringes of the mob, following the main boys around, doing a lot of running up and down, testing the water but not going in the deep end. Because we lived near the ground, however, we were in a perfect position to ambush rival fans and we would spend a lot of time hanging around the streets before and after games, picking off lads who might be bigger and older than us but who we outnumbered. Liverpool, Everton and Leeds were particular targets, because they always brought a lot of fans and there were loads of stragglers

My biggest proper battle in those early days was against Tottenham Hotspur in 1975. They had some decent players and brought a big following up, and at five to three about 100 of their boys infiltrated the Kippax. It was a classic manoeuvre. They gathered behind us at the back of the stand, waited for a pre-arranged signal, then steamed in. We were taken by surprise and surged down the terraces to get away. The crush of bodies at the bottom finally brought us to a halt. A few of us looked at each other and thought, fuck this. The fear gave way to anger that we were being humiliated. We turned and ran back up at them. They had a right go but were heavily outweighed. As more and more City piled in, we chased them up to the top of the Kippax and down the exit stairs, with some of them climbing over the sides of the stairways and jumping off to get away.

Meanwhile, more Tottenham had run into the seats in the Platt Lane end. I came back up to the top of the Kippax to see 400 City chasing them. There was a big fight in the seats and the police waded in but they were no deterrent. There was nothing they could do about several hundred lads brawling. The Cockneys got murdered. They were separated and chased everywhere.

After the match, the entire forecourt outside the ground filled with City fans, waiting for the Spurs. Everyone was fired up because they had dared to come in our end. The Bill kept them in for ages and gave them a massive escort back to the station. That was my first major fight and I was right there, in the forefront.

By this time, City were developing a few young mobs. We had a good firm from Gorton, Wythenshawe had a firm, the likes of Dave Skelly and Jimmy Gittings, and Fallowfield had a good firm, Dave Foulkes and his mates. They all stood in the same part of the Kippax as us. The people I was now hanging around with were mostly older than me and had more experience of football thuggery. I soon picked up on who the boys were. When you went to an away match, you thought, we'll go with them, they're sound. We were still just kids but we were street smart and learning.

Middlesbrough were another team to come on the Kippax, in April, 1977. They brought a few hundred good lads and were fighting all day. They infiltrated our end but were overwhelmed and the cops saved them by turfing them out. After the game, we were brawling in the streets until night-time. The Middlesbrough fans had to walk to town to get their train. We attacked them constantly but instead of running, they stood their ground and took us on. That was the first time I thought, well, they came down here and really stuck at it. That was good. If they stand their ground, you respect them. You also know that when you go to their town, you are going to get it. And you have got to go to their town, because the game is to go to their patch and do it. It's easy kicking arse at your own ground. It's going to an away match and standing with your boys that's the hard thing.

★ ★ ★

Saturday morning, April 23, 1977. I run into our house and up the stairs to Donald's bedroom.

'Donald, get up. There's loads of Scousers down the end of the road. Come on, everyone's in the park. Let's do the Scousers.'

Donald jumps out of bed and looks out of his window. Crowds of fans are already milling around Lloyd Street. Liverpool are playing Everton in an FA Cup semi-final and the Football Association, in its wisdom, has chosen Maine Road as the venue. And if there's one thing we hate, its Scousers.

Donald throws his clothes on and we head downstairs. My mum is waiting at the bottom.

'Donald, love, I want you to go to the bookies and put some money on three horses this afternoon.'

'All right, mam.'

'Take the others with you. But don't go down Denmark Road. You dad says there's a lot of football fans about from Liverpool and some of them might be looking for trouble.'

'Okay, mam.'

We set off for the bookies: me, Donald, Chris and a lad called Doc who my mum took in after his dad threw him out. We cut through the park and cross Great Western Street. A few of our mates are hanging about and they join us. We head down Crofton Street, near the ground.

A small group of Scousers are standing in the road. As we pass, one asks Donald, 'Got any spares, mate?'

He wants tickets but with his Scouse accent the word 'spares' sounds to us like 'spears.' Donald thinks he is taking the piss out of us for being half-castes.

Smack. Donald whacks the guy. I hit another one. Chris, who's only fourteen, joins in and the Scousers scatter. We catch one and weigh him in badly on the floor, then pick him up and throw him in a builder's skip at the side of the road.

We see police coming, so we run back towards Great Western Street, straight into another Scouse mob. We have a quick skirmish and break away, Chris and Doc in one direction and Donald and I in another. The Bill are on our tails. We dive through some alleys and jump over the wall of a derelict house. Donald ducks down and hides. I run into the house and stop, breathless. I can hear the police shouting to each other outside.

'One of them's in the house. Send the dog in.'

Shit. I peep out and see a huge German shepherd pelting towards the house. I run up the stairs and into a back bedroom. I can hear the dog charging after me. I look through the first floor window into the back yard. There's a pile of builders' sand down below. It's either that or an alsatian's teeth in my arse. I climb on to the window sill and jump.

I roll out of the sand and keep running. Thank fuck there's no sign of the dog. I jump over a fence and make it to the park. Then I look back. It's like a scene from The Great Escape: a dozen coppers fanned out in a line chasing me. I keep going until one of them pulls me down. They fill me in and throw me in the back of a van. Donald is already there.

By this time, Chris and Doc have reached Moss Lane. There are police everywhere. They step into a phone box and pretend to make a call. A burly copper pulls open the door.

'You lads wouldn't happen to have been fighting, would you?'

'No, my mam's in hospital and I've just come to phone her,' says Chris. 'We haven't got a phone at home.'

'Oh yeah? What's the number you're ringing then?'

Chris reels off the number of Manchester Royal Infirmary. The copper doesn't know my mum works there. He stares at them for what seems ages, then walks off. They leg it back to our house, where my mum is settling down for a peaceful Saturday afternoon in front of the telly.

'Where's the other two?' she says.

'Don't know,' says Chris.

'Well, as long as they've put my bet on.'

They tuck into some sandwiches and watch a film.

By six o'clock, my mum is getting anxious. Probably wondering what happened to her money.

'Are you sure you don't know where they went?' she asks Chris.

'Er, actually, I don't think they're coming back, mam. They've been arrested.'

The shit hits the fan. The cops keep us in the cells

until 11pm when we are released to our parents. Apparently the bloke in the skip was discovered hours later, unconscious. Donald, who has some previous convictions, is sent to a detention centre for six months. I get a £10 fine. My career as a serious soccer hooligan is under way.

# 3
## *Cool Cats*

THE name Cool Cats came from Cool Cat Sally, a woman in a catsuit in a dodgy seventies film. One of our Donald's nicknames was Sally, because he was always tidying up in the house, and someone stuck the label on our mob. We were one of the first named gangs of the era. Soon the words appeared on graffiti around the area and before long we were known further afield. My uncle Len, who lived in Liverpoool at the time, remembers some young kids playing in the street there and one little ringleader saying to the others, 'We'll be the Cool Cats and you be another gang.' Within a couple of years, there was hardly a soccer thug in the country who hadn't heard of the Cool Cats.

The leader was our Donald. He was a maniac. He was game, loyal and would never run. He was actually far better known than I was as a football hooligan but the later high profile of the Guvnors court case brought all the publicity down on my head. Although only in his teens when the Cool Cats formed, he already had a record for fighting at matches and had been in borstal. This is how he remembers the early days:

*The Cool Cats was a black thing to start with. A lot of the young black and half-caste lads from the area gradually joined together. City wasn't known as a hooligan club but there were a few mobs, like the Beer Monsters and the Beano Boys from Gorton. There was also a big National*

*Front following, Scotty and Co. Although there was a certain amount of mutual respect between us and them, they didn't like us. It was skin deep and there was friction.*

*In the end it spilled over. Our first organised battle as the Cool Cats was against our own supporters. At a home game, our Chris went to the toilets and got done by five or six NF geezers. We had had enough, so after the match we waited for them to leave the ground and as they came out we did them. A lot of black kids then had metal afro combs which folded out. We would sharpen them on the street and use them as weapons. We also stormed the Sherwood Inn, near the ground, which at that time was their pub. There was this fear factor of fifty coloured and half-caste guys. It is a psychological game. Being a half-caste, you are neither white or black, you get it from both sides, so it makes you very tough.*

*We clocked on to using belts with thick buckles as weapons and set up a little firm called the Belt Rippers. We drew pictures of hangmen all over the walls: Hang United and Hang the NF. We were not the biggest crew but we were close knit. If I had to put a year on when it started, I would say 1974, and the Cool Cats ran until about 1983. Our first away game, we walked to Old Trafford. We were fighting all the way. Soon the group grew from fifty to over 100. The NF went everywhere by coach so we decided to get our own coach together. Leeds away was our first trip. We always had white lads integrated into our mob and I remember how the Leeds fans, who are notoriously racist, couldn't understand a black and white mob together. It freaked them out. Some of the white guys included Frank McGory, a big guy from Longsight, Woff, Jimmy Gittings, only small but what a nutter, Mad Roy. I don't know why, but everybody agreed, 'What Donald says, goes.'*

*The Kippax became a fortress. There was the Barmy Army, then the Beer Monsters, then the lunatic fringe like Jimmy Gittings and another lad called Jimmy from Hulme, who was a knife man. He's dead now; he got turned over on a bad drug deal, the front door of this flat was kicked open and he was stabbed. He was a very good lad. Jimmy Gittings was one of the gamest lads I have ever met. For his size he would fight anyone. Frank McGory was a big lad. He was tasty. Then there was a boxer from Longsight called Mark Higgins, he never left my side. Paul Reddy from Salford, he was very tasty. He recently got six months for fighting Birmingham City fans in the riot at the Steve Foster boxing match at the NEC, the big punch-up that was on the telly.*

*We had car stickers made, posters, leaflets, membership cards. I started making a lot of money but nobody could see it. Everybody had to have calling cards: 'You have just been tuned in by the Cool Cats.' Tuned in meant punched, kicked, whacked. If we were bored we used to chase the fans on our own football special, all the scarfers, for a laugh.*

*I have been in court in Oxford, Nuneaton, Walsall, Birmingham Crown twice, Marylebone, Lincoln, Tottenham, Bolton, Carlisle, you name it. I once worked out I have been in thirty-two different courts around the country. We sometimes took coaches to the court cases with all the family and friends. We used to speak backslang, shout it to each other from the cells and really piss off the coppers.*

*The main organisers would meet in the cellar in our house. Sometimes there would be fifteen or twenty of us crammed in there. I started writing to different football grounds, pretending I was a collector and asking for copies* of old match programmes. They usually contained a layout of the ground which we would then use to plan our attacks and decide where to infiltrate. We did it at Arsenal, Leeds, Liverpool, Birmingham City – we did them twice. I got six months there.

Eventually we also used 'sussers.' They would go down two or three days before an away match and suss out the other fans' pubs, meeting places and ambush spots. Everyone would chip in to send them by National Express coach. Then when we went, say, to London, we would park the coach in the city centre and travel the rest of the way by tube because there was more chance of trouble.

Maine Road is one of the worst places to visit, with loads of dark little streets. It wasn't cool to sing or wear a scarf but we had a few little signature chants of our own, such as:

Hit him on the head
Hit him on the head
Hit him on the head with a baseball bat
Oh yeah.

Our biggest offs were against Leeds. Everton was also unbelievable; that was where we really made our name. We took about six coaches. The only firm that day was us and we were representing Manchester. I was about seventeen. Hundreds of them came round a corner near the ground and ran us. We couldn't compete with the numbers. But we re-grouped and I said, 'If anyone runs, that's it. They're getting it off me.'

We did the business but we had loads of casualties on the coach. Anyone who had run wouldn't have been allowed back on the coach. Our mob was never really more than 100 but it was 100 lads that would never run. We *weren't the biggest mob but we were the most disciplined and sometimes with others joining us we got it up to 300.*

Scotty was a top City lad and the leader of a big contingent of Gorton Blues. They had been the main boys, then we came on the scene. Suddenly all these niggers with afros were turning up and they weren't happy about it. Over the years, they jumped a few of our boys and we jumped a few of theirs but really we were all there for City. Racism never bothered me and I didn't hold any grudges.

Being half-caste did mean, however, that you had to be more cautious. At that time, not many black guys went to football matches. With City being in Moss Side, we had a big percentage and when you went away you didn't have to wear a scarf; your skin was your scarf. Rival fans knew that if you were black, you were Moss Side and Man City. If you went somewhere like Liverpool, where blacks didn't go to the football, you stood out a mile. Not that we were too bothered. Trouble was what we were there for. It simply made us tighter knit. We went away in numbers and when you are in numbers, you're strong.

We socialised together and started our own football team. All the young black kids hung about in the Market Centre in town, next to the Arndale. When a Wimpy opened nearby at Piccadilly, it was the first burger bar around and we started mooching about there. It was run by a Souser. He was a nice guy but we drove him half mad. I don't think he quite knew what we were about but he knew were weren't normal lads because he had a torrid time. One day he said, 'Why don't you lot do something useful instead of hanging around here all day?' And so he agreed to sponsor us as a football team: Wimpy FC. We later became Manchester International. Our kit had the name on the back and a badge with a cat, for the Cool Cats, on the front.

We turned out to be pretty good. I think we won the Chorlton League twice and the cup twice. I was a striker. I was fit, didn't smoke and wasn't a big drinker. I scored forty-seven goals one season. Not that I could have made it as a pro. I was just one of those lucky players, there at the right time, and scored two or three a week. Donald was good as well. He had a few trials but they never worked out because of his attitude.

It was funny the way things went. Eventually Donald was offered a job as security guard at the Wimpy. He worked there Thursday, Friday and Saturday nights, keeping any idiots in order. As more young lads got to know who he was, he didn't have to bang too many heads together. His name was enough.

Once we were old enough to go drinking, our other main meeting place became the Parkside, a big pub on Lloyd Street, a few hundred yards from City's ground. On match days they had a collection box on the door, allegedly for Cancer Research, and you had to pay up to get in. We played football for the pub as well, on Sunday mornings, and pool. It became a meeting place during the week as well as match days and was a good place to get all the lads together. If anyone went in that pub on a Saturday that wasn't a City fan, you'd know straight away. We'd do them in, in the pub or outside. The landlord couldn't do anything. He was happy the pub was busy. It was a good boozer, good atmosphere, and the fact that it was more in Fallowfield than

Moss Side meant that lads from that area started to join us.

The Cool Cats had a mystique about them: a close-knit, mixed-race mob from a no-go area. We often teamed up with another firm of about twenty black guys led by Mikey Williams and based around the Robin Hood pub. Most of them lived near us. Mikey is a successful ticket dealer now. Often if we were away and it kicked off, they would come with us or we would go with them. They had a big run-in with the Zulus at Birmingham one time, went in the daytime to the Bull Ring and got their coach smashed up.

A lot of the Cool Cat violence was at Maine Road. Every other week we caused trouble: ambushing police escorts, minibuses, coaches, waiting for them to come past and stoning them, putting the windows through. Sometimes 100 of us would meet in little Whitworth Park to organise our attacks. People will follow you when you're going somewhere, when you stand your ground. Some weeks it was the odd skirmish and other weeks it was full scale battles. The police, who we referred to as the 'dibble' after Officer Dibble in the cartoon *Boss Cat*, or the Five-Oh after one of their radio call signs, didn't catch on for a couple of years. You always knew when it was going to come on top, you could always get off in time, there was that many of you. With hundreds of lads fighting, if you were a bit wily you never got nicked. I was fighting most weeks,, sometimes three or four times a day, with the boys.

Donald also began to hire coaches for away games. We usually took two coachloads, about 120 lads. That's a good-sized firm. If it gets too big you get all the shithouses joining on, the runners. Donald would book a coach for, say, £100, charge a couple of quid a head and make about £100 a coach for himself. Unemployment was high and rising, a lot of people didn't have much money and the coach was a cheap way to travel. You couldn't get a job in our area. Like many others, I never thought about what I wanted to be. I took each day, as I do today, as it comes. We would take cans of beer – no blow in those days – and later we would hide a few baseball bats on the coach.

We would descend on town and cities like a small army, rampaging through shopping centres, wrecking everything in our path. Typical was one game at Stoke City. It isn't far from Manchester and they don't like us at all. They knew about the Cool Cats and were waiting for us in numbers. When you leave Victoria train station, you have to go under a bridge. We came out and were confronted by about 400 lads. They rushed us. We stood. Their arses went. They got halfway and stopped. Then we ran them. As we chased them, we were all chanting, 'The C-o-o-o-l Cats, the C-o-o-o-l Cats.'

In the tunnel, with the echo, it sounded like there were hundreds of us. We ruined them all the way to the ground.

After the match the idea was to get away from the police. We were all making little scheming plans but in the end we opted for the direct approach, got outside and rushed the cops. They didn't know what to do. About 400 broke away and went through Stoke town centre like a cyclone, tipping chairs and stalls over, breaking windows, kicking cars. Then we were back on the train, laughing, everyone saying what they had done and adding a bit on to it. They knew we had been there.

Rampaging was very much the fashion. Manchester

United started it with their Red Army. A few years later, in January, 1980, we played lowly Halifax Town in the third round of the FA Cup. We took about 7,000 fans and if there was ever a riot waiting to happen, that was it. Everyone arrived in town early to go on the piss. They had no boys, which was a bit disappointing. The only problems we had were with the police. They were very worried because there was so many City and they were being heavy-handed to compensate. Their ground, the Shay, is the crappiest I have ever seen. We climbed in over the wall. Of course, City got beat, 1–0. Disgruntled fans threw coins at Tony Book and Malcolm Allison. We all left before the end and hundreds of us did the town centre. It was spontaneous madness. Anything in our way was destroyed. There was no opposition so we took the piss.

Other clubs, however, were a different proposition. One was Birmingham City. This is Donald's recollection:

*The best off I have ever had in my life was at a night match with Birmingham. We took six coaches. One of their boys rang the Brunswick pub and said, 'Tell Donald and the Cool Cats they are old men, they're past it now. If they want it let's meet at the scrap yard near the cemetery.'*

*They knew some of us from England games. We knew it was an ambush. We got near to the meet and sent the suss squad in but they stabbed one of our sussers. We thought, fuck the meet, let's get to the ground and kick it off. We walked straight to their end and went in their seats with twenty-five top lads. Then some lads in the City section gave it away by shouting to us, 'Donald, Donald, give us a wave.' I stood up and waved, the Birmingham realised we were City and it kicked off. But their main boys were still at the cemetery.*

*Like us, Birmingham had a lot of blacks. They were always the first people we went for. If the white guys saw us giving it to their black guys, they'd often get on their toes, because a lot of whites are scared of black guys. When I was outside the ground, with Mike stood next to me, this black geezer came up and, in a broad Brummie accent, said, 'Have you seen the Man City lads?'*

*And I said, 'Yes, we're here,' and whacked him.*

*They used to call me Bullethead because I could butt three or four times in succession. I butted this half-caste at Stoke and pulled out an afro comb and slashed him across the face. The police handcuffed me to a fence and I got kicked to fuck by the Stoke. I got a suspended sentence for that.*

On another occasion, we had a massive kick-off in the Bull Ring in Birmingham city centre. That day, it came on top for us. We were walking through the Bull Ring when hundreds of them came from everywhere. I think even the shoppers joined in. As we were chased, we were kicking everything over. We reached New Street train station and waited there until our football special came in. There was nothing else we could do. Then we got together with the mob from the train, marched through Birmingham and took some revenge.

Inside they separated us, some in the seats and some in the segregated standing area. We went in the seats with Birmingham all around us, chanting. Inevitably it kicked off in the seats and I got caught up against a wall. I got a few smacks and kicks, got dragged onto the floor, and took a bit of a kicking. They had a good mob, Birmingham.

The problem was, we hadn't stood our ground. Football violence is dead simple. If you stay together and nobody runs, you won't get caught on your own. But when a stampede starts – and it just takes one or two to lose their bottle – everyone follows. It's a mind game. If three blokes offer out six, the six start to worry. Every time we got on our toes, four or five of us got our heads kicked in. So we just thought, fuck it, we never run. That became our motto.

After that, it was very rare we ran from anyone. Our numbers went up then because people want to be part of it. We had lads like Dave Foulkes from Fallowfield, he's only small but he'd never run. He could talk a good fight and he'd gee you all up. Dave Israel was the same, a game little lad with loads of confidence. Then there was Jimmy Gittings, from Wythenshawe, one of the gamest lads I've ever known. Those lads were untold.

It's hard to explain to outsiders how we were. We had loyalty and commitment to each other and because most of us had known each other for a long time, we functioned as one, like an army unit. You didn't have to worry about whether or not the lads behind you were going to stand and fight. If it kicks off, you all go together. If someone wants to have a go at you, they have a go at all of you. You don't single one person out. You have us all. And from being a rabble, we started to organise, hanging around town during the day of a match to catch away fans off guard, finding out what times their trains got in.

But while it was all very well doing it against lesser clubs, if you want to be the best, you've got the make your name against the best. And in those days they didn't come any bigger than Manchester United, Liverpool, Everton and Leeds.

# 4

## *Manchester Disunited*

I WAS involved in violence at every Manchester derby game for almost fifteen years. I've known United's boys since I was a teenager: Fez, Benny, Coco, Harry, Sam, Delroy, Tony O, Eddie B . . . these are real boys, top lads, and we have had some right run-ins with them. They would fight you to the end and that's what it's all about. They wouldn't carry weapons, just their fists and whatever came to hand. They're the lads that you respect.

United's firm didn't have a label in the way the Cool Cats did. The Press referred to them all as the Red Army, although that could apply to any United fan. In fact they had many different firms from different areas, including the so-called Cockney Reds, who took a lot of credit for fuck all, as far as I'm concerned. The main United boys I've seen over the years were from Manchester. I think some of them resented the Cockneys' reputation. Sometimes they turned on them; I've been to Old Trafford with City and seen United fans kick off with each other. United draw a lot of lads from places like Collyhurst, Miles Platting, Newton Heath, Ancoats, Salford. These are tough, working class areas. Lads from Wilmslow, or the Home Counties, aren't going to compare to these guys. They live a completely different lifestyle.

One guy who gave me big problems was Harry. He's one of the old boys, a real game fucker. We tangled with him and his mates at every derby game. I think he's hit me a few times, I've hit him a few times. We can talk now, even go for a drink, but years ago I wouldn't be in his company. Even today, a lot of United fans would like nothing better than to do the Guvnors. But they never have. Because they can't find us, they reckon!

United made their name as hooligans in the early 1970s when the Red Army were travelling everywhere in their thousands, invading pitches and smashing places up. No-one can match their numbers on a full turnout. For a while they were the most notorious club in the country. They seemed to be in the papers every weekend, while City were the cosy family club. Yet there had always been friction. In 1970, before a match at Maine Road, the bus crews in Manchester and Salford announced that they wouldn't take supporters because of the possibility of trouble. We won 4–0 and forty-three people were thrown out of the ground.

The first serious trouble I remember was in 1974. We played at Maine Road in March. Forty-five people were injured after running battles around the ground. The second game, on April 27, became famous. It was the last match of the season and if United lost they were relegated. I was only fourteen. I went with Donald and the boys and we were put in a corner, a little section at the front of the Scoreboard Paddock for the City fans, probably about 2,000 of us in a crowd of 57,000. I remember United singing, 'We've got you all surrounded.'

With seven minutes to go, Denis Law scored for us with a backheel. United poured on the pitch, trying to get the game called off. This was how a radio commentator described it:

There are now at least 4–500 supporters on the pitch in front of us. They have their banners and their flags and they're really doing no good at all to the club that they are supposed to follow to all the ends of the earth . . . and now there's a wall of policemen going forward, there must be all of 150 policemen and supporters are falling down; there's one boy in considerable trouble here in front and there are boots being flung, there's kicking going on, there is mayhem down there on the pitch that's meant so much to football. A policeman's lost his helmet and he's in some trouble, a policeman on the floor with three or four supporters on top, and then the wave of policemen come back again and they try to make some sort of sanity and sense out of all this carnage, because really it's the most wicked sight to see anywhere in the world but certainly at a ground which has meant so much, as I say, to this game.

There's one boy being carried off, I see, in the arms of a policeman and another, at least three people being carried off, the St John Ambulance men going out . . . there are now something like fifty or sixty policemen on the pitch, the crowd beginning to disperse, but this game has been abandoned, the last that Manchester United will play in the First Division, certainly for one season, with the local club Manchester City. That's it then, that's the final scene at Old Trafford, a scene really of destruction and viciousness, a scene that one doesn't want to see repeated. From us all at Old Trafford, goodbye.

The match was abandoned with three minutes to go but the result, 1–0, stood and United were down. We had to make our way back up Warwick Road to the 53 bus stop. I was only a kid so I didn't get involved but I know loads of people got hammered. United were going mad but we were elated.

In 1975, we drew them in the League Cup. More than 56,000 saw the game at Maine Road. There was fighting all around the ground, a police sergeant was hit on the head with a brick, two other dibble were hurt and thirty people were ejected after what the papers called 'a general melee.'

In March, 1977, United infiltrated our part of the Scoreboard End at Old Trafford and there was fighting inside and outside the ground. By now, their reputation was so bad that the Minister for Sport ordered all United's away matches to be all-ticket and said terrace tickets should only go to home supporters, although the away fans were allowed in the seats if the clubs wanted them.

This 1977 newspaper report, about the Red Army, could apply to any major mob at that time:

Part of the sub-culture of hooliganism is based on establishing supremacy by taking over the rival team's terraces. It is done like this. In twos and threes, United fans slip virtually unnoticed onto the target terraces. They gradually band together until the gang is fifty or sixty strong. Then they start to chant and wave to the thousands of United fans penned into the opposite end of the ground.

That in itself is considered to be a takeover by some fans, but others insist that it is not complete until the home side's supporters have been out-shouted or seen to come off worst in a gang fight.

There is a certain comformity of dress among the hooligan fans which has earned them the nickname of the Red Army among the media. In the uniform, the scarf – traditionally a garment for keeping necks warm – is worn knotted around the wrist like a manacle. No-one knows why, except that it can be waved in a crowd without the risk of losing it. Trousers, usually white or cream, are invariably baggy and end several inches above the ankle. Tartan stripes down the legs are optional. The legs end in a pair of large, cushion-soled boots.

Whatever happened to the good old woollen bob-cap and wooden rattle?

We didn't give a fuck about their reputation and gave them a taste before the derby at Old Trafford on September 30, 1978. There was a pitched battle between about eighty boys when we attacked the Brewers Arms pub off Market Street in town. Iron bars and lumps of concrete were thrown through the windows and chairs and tables were overturned and smashed. At the game, there was an incident which led to a famous picture of a City fan being escorted around the pitch with a dart stuck in the top of his head. Hamrick Bryan was a student who lived on our road, Acomb Street, although I didn't know him. A United fan threw the dart into the City section and it embedded in the top of his skull. The guy who chucked it got off in court when he said the dart had been thrown at him first, had hit his hand, and he instinctively grabbed it and threw it back!

Although we had no end of run-ins with United, it was rare that our main mobs actually came face to face. This was one occasion, as Donald recalls:

*United had a very good mob that day but we had leathered them all around before the match. When we came out at the end, their firm was waiting, all their top men. They walked in front of us, with both sides waiting for a chance to get at each other. They had a black guy who was dancing about doing kung fu and he kicked me in the head. I did kick-boxing so we were having a bit of a toe-to-toe and the police split us up.*

*We reached White City but the local Man United fans, the Mancs, seemed a bit apprehensive. They may have been worried about repercussions because we used to say that town belonged to us and if it came on top for us at the game we would always get revenge in the town centre at night. But the Cockney Reds came in and had a go and we slapped them.*

*Finally one of the top Mancs couldn't stand it any more. He came over to me, said, 'I've had enough of this,' and butted me in the mouth. I whacked him back and a lad called Jimmy, one of our knifemen, stabbed him in the arse. We eventually marched all the way back to town, to the Wimpy, sticking together all the way. A couple of the lads went in a car to get some tools and passed them to us and we stormed United round town. Later we said we'd meet them at 2am at Piccadilly. There was a big battle between Hulme and Ancoats and a few lads were stabbed.*

*We had lots of ploys to attack United. If you supported them and you were from Moston, Blackley, Collyhurst, that side of town, you had to get the number fifty-three bus, which went through Moss Side. We would stone the buses. We wouldn't touch them going to the match, when it was daylight, but at night it was dark and they had to come back through Whitworth Park. We would put bins across Great Western Street to stop them. It got so bad that they received police escorts. Then we changed our tactics and went to Longsight/Wilmslow Rd.*

There was mayhem at the fixture at Maine Road the following February. A policeman got a dart stuck in his back, there were scuffles breaking out all over the terraces, three fans were hit by flying bottles and a beer can, the match was held up when someone threw a smoke canister on the pitch and police ejected 122 fans. We left the ground at the same time as their 'end.' Thousands of them rushed us. We stuck together like glue and we got onto Kippax Street, about 200 of us, with this massive mob behind us, running at us all the time. We'd skirmish, retreat, skirmish, retreat. The police had the dogs and horses out, trying to separate us. We went deep into our territory in Moss Side but 1,000 United stayed on our tail. There was a kid from Jamaica who had been over for just two weeks and who wanted to join the Cool Cats. He stabbed one of the United, got arrested and was later deported. But being so outnumbered, more and more of our mob began to peel away and vanish.

Donald was leading those of us that were left:

*By the time we reached Whitworth Park, we were down to about forty, being followed by a mob of about 300. United kept making runs at the park but the police were separating us and we were laughing. Some of the nippers in our street prepared with milk bottles. We reached the shop at the corner of our road and all the black guys playing cards came out to help us. Most of our lot were just teenagers. It kicked off again.*

One of United's top boys is Paul D. He is a friend of mine now. He had a tough background, like me, being one of seven brothers from Lower Broughton in Salford. Five of them support City and the other two United. Paul is the same age as our Donald. This is his story of how he became a hooligan and his view of the City-United rivalry:

They say Ryan Giggs was showing his football skills at the age of seven. I did my first burglary at seven. I became a professional villain in the same way he became a professional footballer. But I paid for it. I was in approved schools up to the age of eighteen. Three months before my eighteenth birthday, they called me in and said they would have to let me go, but my chances of making it on the outside were one in 100. When I came out, all I knew was violence. You had to be a fighter in the approved schools.

Then one of my friends asked me to go to a football match, Manchester United away against Newcastle. I had never been to a game before. Just before the end of the match, twenty of us got thrown out. The next thing, the final whistle had gone and 3,000 Newcastle came pouring round the corner towards us. The rest of the United were still locked inside. What happened next, the violence, having to run and having to battle, was, by the time we got back to the coaches, so exciting that I was on a total high. That was it for me.

I don't think I knew what offside meant until I had been going for four years. I didn't really have a clue. For me it was all about total violence. From Liverpool came the trend to have your violence before and after the game and dip pockets during. Football hooligans realised that there was money to be earned. There was a famous occasion when United were playing in a Cup final in London and a group did a jewellers out of £25,000-worth of gear. That was the last big earner.

United had a huge following but when the dipping came in, when people started to go away to earn money, that's when people started to stand out, and that was where the name the Main Boys came in. Other people called United's fans the Red Army but we always called the mass of fans the Barmy Army. So you had the Barmy Army and the Main Boys.

I have never been to Maine Road and entered the United section of the ground. I have always gone in the City end. United's fans would always be put in the far right hand corner of the Kippax, as you look at the pitch. But every year, there used to be fifty United fans on the Kippax, at the bottom, next to the other United fans but in with the City. You knew it would always kick off in there. So we used to get in there quarter of an hour before the start. City fans would arm themselves with loads of bricks and lob them into the crowd. There were lots of injuries.

With United being so well supported, after the match it was hard for United's main mob to find City. City's main mob would be fighting and beating up the Barmy Army. They'd be having a fantastic day while we were out just looking to fight their main firm. We're not interested in City's Barmy Army because they're total idiots, hats on their heads, scarves wrapped round them. But it was hard for us to really get into City.

United don't rate City for that reason. We have hooligans coming from all over the country. While

City might have fifty main hooligans, we might have 2,000 and you can't imagine that fifty looking for our 2,000, our main team. We always had our fun when we went away because at home we were untouchable.

I remember going to Maine Road on one occasion with my brother Mark, who supports City. They have a bookies in the ground, Mark was putting a bet on and I shouted to him, 'Put a tenner on United to win 3–0.'

All these City fans heard me and were staring at us, giving us the evil eye. Mark owed me £300 at the time, so to get his own back for me showing him up, he put the lot on United to win 3–0, then handed me the slip. When the first United goal went in, I stood up in the City seats and cheered. I was surrounded by City fans shouting, 'Sit down, Munich.'

I had a bit of a row, two of my brothers came running over and the police pulled me out for my own safety. I went round to the United part of the ground, told the stewards that I had been sent to see a police officer and they let me in. Then United scored another... and another. With ten minutes to go, Giggs broke through. I was begging him not to score – and he didn't. I came in at 16–1. Mark phoned me up when I got home and his exact words were, 'You stuffy, Munich, red bastard.'

It didn't always go that well. I was at the game in 1989 when we lost 5–1. A hundred United fans went in the City end, there was fighting, the game was stopped and the United players couldn't get it together after that. They just went to pieces. I left at half-time because I couldn't take any more. I always thought City were a joke but after that I hated them.

My brothers are raving lunatics. They are notorious at City. One of them, Bradley, it is nothing for him to walk out of the City stadium naked. He's been shot, axed, stabbed, he doesn't care. He had a fight once with Harry, one of United's main boys, at Old Trafford. Because he was my brother, they were pulled apart and our Brad was thrown out without serious injury. But he will walk anywhere with a City shirt on. When a man has been shot, a good hiding is nothing to him. He's a character.

I first heard of Mike and his brothers in the early eighties, at the time football violence became organised. I don't remember any particular fights with them because to me, a fight's just a fight; I don't keep cuttings or make notes. The only time we had trouble with City was when they came to Old Trafford. Then we knew who their main mob was. They always used to arrive five minutes after the kick-off, for some reason. United have always hated City. At the Liverpool derbies, the Scousers can stand side by side. It's impossible to do that at a Manchester derby.

I was at Middlesbrough when United won the Premiership and I'm standing on my seat next to this guy who's got an earpiece in, listening to the radio. When the match finishes, everyone cheers and the team walk round the pitch with the trophy. Five minutes later, this bloke jumps up and cheers. I said, 'Fucking hell, mate, you're a bit slow.'

He said, 'City have just got relegated.'

He had more of a cheer at City going down than he did for United winning the League. That shows the hatred between City and United. I think the more hatred comes from City. All you get out of some of them is 'Munich.' A City fan can never put up an argument against United because what have they won compared to us? Even when they were winning things, United were still the biggest club.

Bollocks.

There was more trouble when we played them in September 1985, after coming up from Division Two. About 2,000 United got on the Kippax, because a lot of City season ticket holders had touted their tickets. United scored an early penalty and when their Kippax contingent jumped up they were attacked by the City fans. The Five-Oh had to march all 2,000 fans out of the end, along the touchline and into an empty enclosure. That was the first game in the north-west in which the use of police video cameras led to a successful prosecution. They filmed the fighting and a City fan from Salford was picked out at our next home game. He got 100 hours community service for breach of the peace. It was a sign that police tactics were changing but nobody took any notice. Perhaps we should have, in the light of what was to come.

The worst fight I was involved in against United was at a pub called the Whalley, in Whalley Range. We were playing them at Old Trafford and a mate of mine called Vinny, who later killed himself, was a United fan. Someone said to him as a bit of a joke, 'Tell United we'll meet them in the Whalley, we'll be there at two o'clock.'

So of course, he fucking told them all, didn't he? We walked through Hulme with a firm of 200. We got to the Whalley and had just had a pint when the windows came in. About 600 of them had turned up. We were surrounded. The Whalley got wrecked. There were bricks and bottles coming through every window. Some of them ran in with scaffold tubes. One of our lads, Mad James, who really was mad, ran outside and attacked them on his own. He got mangled. I came out on the steps and Fez, I have known him for years, we're mates, he had a big fucking belt in his hand and we were fighting each other. And we used to know each other dead well; we played for the same football team on a Saturday mornings. Come the derby day, we didn't give a fuck. We stood them off – we had to. We managed to get out of the bar into the car park. Everyone was in a right mess. It was horrible. I thought, I'm going to fucking die here. Eventually the TAG boys turned up. We were escorted to the ground with United attacking us all the way. By the time we got there, half our mob had had enough and sneaked away.

Often, we had ambushes waiting for United when they returned from away games, or vice versa. We had murders in town. We would wait, thirty or forty strong, for their trains to come in and then kick fuck out of them as they came out of the station, as they waited for buses or when they stopped in a pub for a drink. That has been going on for twenty years and still goes on now. Then we'd come all the way back from a long trip and find United waiting for us. Sometimes the fighting continued after the clubs had shut in the early hours.

Even though I can drink with a lot of their boys now, if I went in the wrong pub at the wrong time, someone would say, 'There's that fucking Francis, the Guvnor,' and they would try to do me in. So I don't bother. On occasions, I've been to United games with some of their boys, but only very rarely because there are always people that want to do you in. I'd be with certain members of their firm and others would be glaring at me. If the crowd turns on you, you're cooked. I went three or four times and didn't feel happy about it. I never could sing, 'Glory, glory, Man United,' for one thing. I did go, however, when Everton played at Old Trafford in an FA Cup replay. I helped them to do the Scousers in, but then everyone hates Scousers, don't they?

# 5
## Scousers

THE enmity between Manchester and Liverpool football fans in the 1970s and 1980s was the worst in English football. Only Celtic–Rangers in Glasgow could compare. With the two cities being just thirty-five miles apart, Liverpool and Everton always brought their full firms to Manchester and we and United always took ours there. Mayhem was guaranteed.

The Scousers brought the knives out: they started the stabbings and slashings at football matches. There had always been the odd knifing incident but it was rare. The Scousers made the name Stanley knife notorious for more than cutting up carpets. One trick they had was to put a matchstick between two razor blades and tape them together, so that when they cut the skin it was harder to stitch. When numbers were equal, they'd usually run, but if they got hold of one or two of you, they'd carve you up and laugh about it.

In our experience, Everton were the gamer fighters, while Liverpool had more numbers, like United. Lots of out-of-towners follow Liverpool, while Everton are more like us, local lads. In the years I followed City, we had more serious violence at Everton. Both adopted the same tactics whenever they came to Manchester: arrive early in the morning and head for the Arndale Centre to rob the shops and look for trouble.

Liverpool, of course, were the most successful team in Europe at that time and, on the pitch, our record against them was dire. Between 1975 and 1983, when we were relegated, we played them sixteen times in the League. We won two, drew one and lost thirteen, conceding forty goals. The rivalry had always been there but it escalated in the late seventies because Liverpool were so cocky. There was also mass unemployment in both cities and a lot of bored young men who looked forward to the weekend as the only excitement in their lives.

My first trip to Liverpool was with the Cool Cats and I immediately noticed that it was a bad place to go if you were black. You stood out a mile. There has always been a racist element there – bananas were thrown at John Barnes when he played in his first Merseyside derby – and you didn't see many blacks on the terraces. The usual Scouse method of sussing outsiders is to ask them the time and listen to their accent when they reply; they didn't need to do that with us.

We had so many fights, I can't remember them all. Every time we played them it was one long battle. In 1978, City's offical coach firm for supporters, Fingland's, refused to run any more trips to Merseyside because of damage. In March, 1980, a City fan was stabbed by mistake by our own fans at Anfield. That October, what the papers called 'rampaging soccer gangs' fought all over Manchester when Liverpool came to play. It was made worse by a load of Chelsea who stopped off in Manchester on their way to play Bolton. As usual, the Scousers raided loads of shops near the ground and even beat up a young newspaper seller and his two brothers.

But all of this was just a warm up for the 1980–1 season, probably the most violent I can remember. Not only did we play Liverpool and Everton twice each in the League, we also played Liverpool twice in the League Cup semi-final and Everton twice in the FA Cup quarter-final. It was war. Each battle seemed to get worse, to the stage where every other coach operator in Greater Manchester joined Fingland's and refused to run match-day trips to Liverpool.

The first off was Liverpool at home on October 4. They arrived with a mob of 400 at Oxford Road station. 'None of the supporters were wearing scarves,' said a police spokesman. 'They were out to cause trouble.' These were the original scallies, dressed in the gear that was to become the 'casual' fashion, some of it plundered on away trips to European cities. As usual, they headed for Market Street, terrorising shoppers and looking for whatever they could snatch. They continued when they reached the ground, robbing and wrecking a sweetshop in Claremont Road. We were waiting for them. There was a huge kick-off outside the ground, broken up when the mounted cops launched what I can only describe as a cavalry charge.

There was little evidence of seasonal goodwill when we played Everton on Boxing Day at Goodison. United played Liverpool on the same day and there were more clashes there. Then came our League Cup semi-final against Liverpool, with the first leg at home on January 14.

Before the game, a young lad was slashed across the face by Scousers at the Arndale Centre. Word passed around and we were out for revenge. Many Liverpool fans parked their cars in the side streets near the Claremont pub and after the game we headed over there to see if any had stopped at the chippy on the corner. We spotted a handy little mob who must have come on a coach or in a van and fifty of us steamed into them. They ran down Claremont Road and into the same shop that they had wrecked the previous October. What happened next was later described by the lady who ran the shop:

More than twenty Liverpool fans suddenly rushed into the shop. They wrecked the place when they last played City and we thought we were in for the same treatment. But this time they were on the run from City fans. They said if we didn't let them stay under cover in the shop they would take it apart. They were all men, not youngsters, but I still grabbed one around the neck. He was really scared and said he was just looking for somewhere to hide.

Then a massive gang of City supporters gathered outside. There were fights going on in the road and in the shop doorway and the Liverpool fans were grabbing bottles and throwing them outside. They said some of the City fans were armed with knives. We dialled 999 but the police didn't turn up. They said they had enough to cope with already. One young bobby who had been directing traffic came over to try to do something but he had no chance. There were just too many of them.

My mother got in the thick of it and tried to get them out but she only succeeded in breaking her watch and bracelet. We are all lucky none of us was badly hurt. The fight stopped as quickly as it had started and after ten minutes they all disappeared.

The Scousers tried to stand us off but were bombarded. Most of them were terrified, but who wouldn't be, trapped in the middle of Moss Side with a bunch of animals attacking you? The shop was wrecked, four or five Scousers got caught and leathered and the rest scattered and legged it. It wasn't a big crew of them, so it was nothing to brag about.

Knives were being pulled all over the place when we played them in the second leg at Anfield on February 10. Five people needed hospital treatment for stab wounds inside the ground; two were hurt so badly that the police said they were lucky not to have had two murders on their hands. 'We think there may have been several more slashing incidents which were not reported,' said an officer. Fingland's had lifted their coach ban for the game but immediately reinstated it after suffering thousand of pounds-worth of damage to their vehicles. Thirty people were arrested, most of them in the ground, about half from City. Most of the City were done for having offensive weapons, including carpet knives, flick knives, iron bars, baseball bats, a cricket bat, a hockey stick, a pick handle, a knuckleduster and a chain. All they got was fines.

The next game, the FA Cup sixth-round at Goodison, was the heaviest of the lot. Again, there were no coaches, because of the fear of reception committees. The Scousers were great ones for stoning the buses. City's club secretary, Bernard Halford, wrote to Merseyide Police asking them to provide a convoy for a fleet of coaches from the end of the M62 but got no reply. Frank Palmer of Mayne Coach Hire told the Press, 'Our coaches have been bombarded with everything hooligans can lay their hands on.'

That meant that the 13,000 City fans would be travelling by rail or car. Many were going on a 560–seat football special, due to leave Manchester Victoria at noon. We knew, however, that it would be heavily policed. Instead we caught the earlier scheduled service:

Rival Manchester City and Everton soccer fans fought in the streets of Liverpool this afternoon.

There were ugly scenes at Lime Street station when the first train load of about 100 City supporters arrived for the FA Cup quarter-final tie. As they were leaving the station, they were charged by a mob of thugs and skirmishes broke out. Platform luggage trolleys were used as battering rams.

It is believed that the attackers were Everton and Liverpool FC fans who had joined forces to do battle against the rivals from Manchester. Sirens blared as police reinforcements were on the scene within minutes. A mob of about 200 youths were later cornered and surrounded by police on the steps of Liverpool Museum.

One officer at the scene said: 'It's always the same when any Manchester fans come to Liverpool. The Liverpool and Everton supporters team up and go looking for trouble.'

The entire Liverpool police force was on stand-by ready for an invasion of an estimated 13,000 Manchester fans.

Everyone was keyed up on the train journey, giving it the usual, 'Right lads, all stick together, no runners.' We pulled into Lime Street, left the platform and walked into the main concourse. There were a few Old Bill scattered around. Suddenly, we were ambushed from all sides. It was bedlam: women screaming, luggage flying, people cowering in terror. Even with dogs, the police had no control.

We managed to get out of the station and down towards Liverpool Museum. And there, on the steps by the statues, were hundreds and hundreds of Scousers, waiting. We were facing Everton and Liverpool combined. We would never have accepted United boys in our firm but they seemed to have a good relationship with each other. I thought, this is it. We're going to get done. They started lobbing bottles across the road as a prelude to a full-frontal attack. But there was no way we were going back to that station. We stood our ground and had it with them – and the Scousers started getting on their toes. One of them ran into the path of a bus. He hit the deck and some of the lads booted him on the floor.

The cops were there in numbers now but we still faced a long walk to the ground. I had a woollen scarf pulled up to hide my face and was leading the firm. Scousers were all around us, going, 'Come 'ead, lads, come 'ead.' They kept trying to slip through the police escort to get into us and we kept slapping them back. We had main boys at the front and main lads at the back to keep the firm together.

A car pulled up and two blokes jumped out. CID. One says, 'Hey you, fucking nigger, don't hide yer fucking face here, we know who you are. Pull your fucking mask down, you.'

I took my scarf off and put it in my pocket. The copper said, 'Keep walking, you're going to get what you fucking deserve when you get up the road. We're off now. You're going to get hammered by the Scousers.'

They got back in the car and followed us at a crawl. We walked all the way to the ground, 400 of us by now, escorted by sixty police and about 600 Scousers walking beside us. Finally we came down a hill towards the ground. At the bottom were hundreds of fans. No-one was wearing colours and we weren't sure who they were. The word went round, 'Fuck this, we'll have them all,' and with that we got on our toes and broke through the front of the police escort. The Scousers trailing us thought we were running from them and came charging down after us. To the mob waiting at the bottom, it looked like 1,000 City fans pouring towards them, when in fact it was 400 City with 600 Everton behind. We were moving at jogging pace and on the way down all you could hear was Scousers panicking, yelling, 'The fucking Mancs are here, the Mancs are here.' They scattered like mice. It was brilliant.

The score was 2–2 and the return was set for the following Wednesday. We prepared; we had every kid we knew in Moss Side and Fallowfield collect bottles and stash them for an ambush while we waited at the Parkside. We were expecting their main firm; we had been there and done it and now it was up to them.

As usual, Everton came early, but they made the mistake of arriving in groups of ten and twenty, rather than in one big firm. It was a bit of a farce. We took the piss and leathered them all over the place. Some were done right outside the ticket office. There was also a bit of a skirmish outside the Platt Lane, where all their fans were, but nothing like we expected. The knives came out in Manchester that night and I think three or four of them were stabbed. That was our response to them using knives: fight fire with fire.

I never carried a blade but by then we had lads called jibbers who did. A jibber, which can also mean a scrounger, is a person who carries a weapon, often an ordinary wood-handle kitchen knife with a piece of cardboard folded over for a scabbard and hidden down their trousers, not in their jacket, in case they get searched. They are usually only small knives, a couple of inches long, so when you jib someone you can't do much damage, just jib them up their arse, make a wound and put them down but don't kill them. We had a few jibbers, mainly younger lads.

I got to know a few of the Scouse boys by sight but not by name. We didn't talk to Scousers. The Yankee Bar near Lime Street station was Liverpool's hangout. We went in there one year, about fifty of us, arriving early before their mob. They were not happy. Eventually the street outside filled up with them and they started smashing up the doorway to get in. The police came, got us out, took us back to the station and put us on the next train back to Manchester. We didn't even get to the ground.

They were great robbers, the Scousers. One year a load of Everton even made a detour into Manchester before a pre-season friendly at Oldham to rob Hurley's sports shop at Piccadilly. Hurley's was a bit of a magnet for the casuals because it sold all the trendy golfing clobber and all the designer labels.

In September, 1982, the rivalry grew worse, if anything, after Everton fans carved up a Man United lad called Jobe Henry outside Old Trafford. Jobe, who was nineteen at the time, was a mate of my brother's and a handy lad, a bit of a boxer. He needed 200 stiches in cuts down his back when he got caught by a gang near the swing bridge. Another United fan was slashed nearby. Even City fans were sick when Liverpool had a banner made up that said, 'Jobe, how's you arse?'

They didn't care, though. I remember one game against them at Maine Road in April, 1983. It was a Monday night match and we were outside the Kippax, about fifty of us, talking. Liverpool came round the corner and we had a right set-to. They pulled out blades. None of our jibbers were around so we had to get on our toes. After a bit of a chase we stopped, ran back, caught a Scouser and gave him a kicking, but by that time there were two City fans slashed from ear to mouth, in that charge.

My last major battle with the Scousers was in the Guvnors era. We drew Everton away in the Littlewoods Cup quarter-final in January, 1988, just three weeks before we were all finally arrested. It was a Wednesday night and we went on the train. We came out of Lime Street station, walked around the corner and 200 lads suddenly poured out of the pubs nearby. Many of them pulled blades. I was standing next to a mate called Pete Frith and in the blink of an eye his mouth was ripped open with a cut-throat razor. It was horrible; his cheek was hanging off. He carries the scar to this day. We retreated back into the station, grabbed metal bins and luggage trolleys, anything, and ran back at them. It took us an hour and a half to get to the ground and we were fighting non-stop.

After the game (we lost 2–0), 100 of us stayed in the ground for ages, singing and fucking about, winding up the Scousers. Finally the ground emptied, the lights went out and the Bill told us to go. We came outside and the buses to take fans back to Lime Street had all gone.

Anfield, like Maine Road, is surrounded by little streets, and it was pitch dark. We set off walking. Around the corner came 300 Mickey Mousers.

'Get the nigger! Get the nigger!'

The only black faces were me and our Chris. It was shit or bust. We made a stand. A lot of us put our hands in our jackets, pretending we had blades, to keep them at bay. As the Five-Oh turned up, we made a break for it. Most of the lads jumped on a bus; the doors were shutting as I got there, with a pack of Scousers on my tail, and just managed to prise them open and get on. The police finally stopped us and we were taken to Edgehill station. We had missed the last train. The police locked us in a compound at the station and British Rail had to get a train out for us. We got home at 1am. I'll remember that night forever.

# 6
## *We Hate Leeds*

ONE of the most popular football songs goes, to the tune of The Dambusters, like this:

> We all hate Leeds and Leeds and Leeds
> Leeds and Leeds and Leeds
> Leeds and Leeds and Leeds
> We all fucking hate Leeds.

They're not the most imaginative lyrics, but you get the picture. And while I was a paid-up member of the hate-Leeds brigade, I always loved going there. You were guaranteed a major ruck. Whatever anyone says about them, those Yorkshire pie-munchers have got some boys and they're always up for it. Elland Road is my favourite place for a battle. Along with United and the Scousers, we considered Leeds our major rivals and, from my earliest days as a hooligan, we reserved a special welcome for them at Maine Road. We knew they would reciprocate when we went there.

Like City, Leeds under Don Revie were one of the big teams in British football in the late sixties and early seventies. They had a reputation for being a very dirty team which, coupled with their success, made them unpopular. Football fans tend to resent other teams doing well; later it became, 'We hate Liverpool' and now it's, 'We all hate Man Utd.' Added to this, for Mancunians, was the traditional Lancashire–Yorkshire rivalry, while, for their part, Leeds particularly disliked Man United, who were always seen as more glamorous, even when Leeds had the best side in the country. They were always singing 'Munich' songs, about the 1958 air crash. Like United, their fans wanted to attract a reputation and eventually the media dubbed Manchester-Leeds games 'The Wars of the Roses.'

We had our own grudge against them. On September 29, 1979, at Elland Road, they beat up a seven-year-old City fan. His dad, who was thirty-three, had taken him to an away match as a birthday treat. They had scarves on, had been in the seats, which was where all the normal fans went in those days, and had waited inside the ground to let the home fans disperse before they left. They still weren't safe. When they left the ground, after we had won 2–1, they were jumped by thirty lads. A skinhead smacked the little kid in the face, busting his nose and lip, then they kicked shit out of his dad as he tried to protect his son with his body. The dad was pictured in the papers the next Monday with a head like a balloon. When he had complained to the nearest copper, he was told it was his own fault for taking a kid to the match.

Now that was out of order. Look for a kick-off with the boys, fine, the lads who want a fight. You can tell them by the way they dress and behave. But you don't kick the dads and mams in. Leeds made a habit of that sort of thing. A few years later, thirty of them did the same to a Manchester University student who was walking along minding his own business, not even going to the match. He was knocked out, hit on the head with a bottle while he was unconscious and woke up in hospital.

My first game at Leeds was when Wille Donachie, the Scottish international, played for City. I think he scored his only goal for us against Leeds. He was rubbish. I was about sixteen, in my Dr Marten boots. I went on the train with my mate Gan Bellows. He plays in a band now, Light of the World. When we were sitting in the carriage, he said, 'You're going to get your head kicked in dressed like that.'

'No chance, mate.'

We had a bet on it. We were with a group of about fifty and thought we were the business but we got lost going to the match and had to run a couple of times. In the ground we were in two pens, about 800 City, and I thought, we're the boys, this mob will never get done. Then we got outside and City ran everywhere. I was chased and got a bit of a kicking at the train station, a smack and a bloody nose. I didn't fight back. Sixteen years old, on your own, you don't want to know.

I got on the train and Gan was there, laughing his bollocks off because he'd won his bet. I had white skinners at the time and they had boot marks all over them. I sat in the carriage on the way back with my nose all over my face, thinking, bastards. But things like that made me want to go again because I thought, the next time, we'll come down here with a right firm and have you over. Their boys would be out because they knew that when they came to Manchester, City or United, everyone turned out. They came to Maine Road in mass numbers and they always fought, they never ran.

Pitch invasions were a big thing back then, as Donald recalls.

*We were losing in the FA Cup at Elland Road in 1977*

*and Leeds were stoning us from the Lowfield Road. Dennis Tueart was taking a corner. Someone said, 'The only way this match is going to be saved is if it's abandoned.' So a guy called Mikey lay on the floor and pretended he had been hit by a stone. We went to the St John Ambulance, who opened the gate to take him out and we stormed onto the pitch. But the ref wouldn't stop the game.*

We went as the Cool Cats in January, 1978, again in an FA Cup match. There were more than 8,000 City there in a crowd of 38,000. There was all sorts of mayhem. Leeds were losing and invaded the pitch, stopping the match for sixteen minutes. Then an Asian guy ran on and punched their striker, Joe Jordan. We were all singing, 'Jordan is a wanker.' He was pointing at the City fans with his head, as if to say he was going to head a goal, and then he came across and scored. But we beat them 2–1 and they were later fined £1,000 for the pitch invasion.

At the time, they were building a new subway at Leeds and we had to pass through it to get back to the train station. About 800 of us were ambushed. They always bricked you and reaching the station was murder. On this occasion, everyone panicked because of the sheer weight of stones and bottles. We ran onto a playing field and fought for ten minutes before the police came. I have to say they did us that day.

Usually we escaped the escorts by taking an early train or going by coach, meeting up in a pre-arranged pub. For local games like Leeds we would drive over the night before and suss out the best pubs in the area, tell people where to go when they get off the train, sort out the 'meet.' If you were lucky, your coach wouldn't get picked up coming off the motorway by the police. Then we could get together and go hunting.

We next played them in September, 1979, when the little kid was battered. About five coachloads of us went, parked up in town, met a massive firm and simply overpowered them in the middle of the street. Again, there were bricks flying everywhere. This time it was Leeds's turn to run. A lot of lads then wore full-length, black leather coats and I remember one black kid from Leeds, in one of these trench coats, making a stand on his own. He got knocked out and his coat was ripped off his back.

The tally for the day was dozens injured, a police car trashed and thirty-three people arrested. One City fan was still in hospital months later. A Manchester MP, Charles Morris, complained to Home Secretary Willie Whitelaw about what happened at the ground. He said, 'City fans were positioned below Leeds supporters in the south stand. They were sitting targets and were constantly bombed with a variety of missiles. Leeds fans were allowed out of the ground first but they laid in wait for City supporters making their way to the railway station and coaches.'

That sort of thing was par for the course at Elland Road. Obviously there was going to be trouble when they came to our place in February, 1980. This time a party of Manchester MPs visited Maine Road to see how the police handled the crowds, after complaints from their constituents who were terrified of getting their homes wrecked. While the MPs were praising the 'efficiency' of the police at the ground, we were battling 200 Leeds in the Arndale Centre.

It was during this period that I was arrested at Elland Road. I was about twenty and was in the away supporters' end, with a kind of no man's land between us and the Leeds. Their fans are very racist and were directing chants at the Cool Cats. So I jumped the fence and ran at the Leeds on my own. I was tackled by the police before I could reach them and was frogmarched out. The lads were all singing, 'We'll see you again, we don't know when, goodbye Mickey, goodbye.'

As I was dragged past the seats, the old gits were all spitting at me, shouting, 'You scum, you yob.' They put me in a cell beneath the stand and I missed the match. I was charged with a public order offence. At quarter to five, the final whistle, the dibble let me go, right underneath the Leeds end. I came out of the ground into the middle of a sea of Yorkies, all milling around, saying, 'Come on, let's do the City.'

I had no choice but to keep my head down and go with the flow, pretending I was one of them. Leeds went towards the City end, waited for them to come out and then chased them up this hill. I saw a little half-caste kid with a Leeds scalf on and walked beside him, acting like I was his big brother, but four lads sussed me out. They asked me the time, I told them and they must have realised I was a Manc. They waited until I reached the train station, where there was a British Rail guard saying, 'Anyone going to Manchester, go to your right, any other destination, to your left.'

I went to the right, got to the top of the stairs and I felt this whack on the back of my head. The next thing I was getting kicked to fuck on the stairs. I'd made it all the way to the station without a scratch only to get battered yards from safety. A police woman came through with a truncheon and saved me from getting done in proper. Back in Manchester, I met the lads in a pub and we had a good laugh about it. I wound them up something chronic about me chasing them with the Leeds fans. 'We chased you lot everywhere, you all got legged, you wankers.'

Because of the lively welcomes we got there, we always reserved our best reception committees for Leeds. Typical was this newspaper report in April 1985:

Soccer hooligans went on the rampage in Manchester centre after City's clash with Leeds United. A convoy of twenty-five buses carrying the Yorkshire fans from the Maine Road ground was attacked as it neared Victoria Station.

Despite a heavy police escort, eleven buses were damaged and there were thirteen arrests for public order offences. A Greater Manchester Transport spokesman said seventeen windows were smashed and twenty seats were hurled from the buses. All those charged will appear at the magistrates' court on April 23.

At Victoria several gates to the platform were damaged as the crush of fans pushed forward. Police closed New Bridge Street outside the station for forty-five minutes while the buses were unloaded.

Earlier at the ground an eighteen-year-old Leeds fan was stabbed in the back of his thigh and had twelve stitches in hospital. The identity of his attacker was not known.

The bus drivers were ordered by the cops to keep going even when their windows had been caved in, which was just as well for the bastards on board.

Of course, they did our buses as well. We went with

150 Guvnors in the mid-eighties, when we were both in Division Two. We parked at a pub and were fighting all day. When we returned, my coach had been smashed to bits and had been towed away by the police, who told us to get the train. Instead we went into Leeds town centre for a drink. Most of the scum had gone home for their pies for tea and there was no-one about. We went into a hotel bar by the police station. Everyone else decided to go but fifteen of us stayed behind for another drink. Finally we went to the station and were in the diner there when there was a big shout of 'United! United!'

We walked outside, grabbing knives and forks to protect ourselves, and met 200 members of the Leeds Service Crew. This old security guard tried to keep them away from us. No chance, old boy. It came on top. They rushed the restaurant and we jumped onto the rail tracks. Me and a mate called Tony jumped up on a platform and scrambled onto a train.

We could see a lad called Donald Farrer being chased down the tracks. Farrer is a lunatic. A black lad from Middleton, just north of Manchester, he has been nicked dozens of times at football. In fact he once had sessions with a psychotherapist in an attempt to cure him of his compulsion to attend matches, which goes to prove that anyone who follows Man City should have his head examined. He has been in the papers loads of times, has been booted out of foreign countries and is on the National Football Intelligence Unit blacklist. People called him Mad Donald or Daft Donald. He had his own little firm but often came with us.

On this occasion, he must have regretted it. He was rugby-tackled by this big Leeds monster and fell on the tracks and they were all around him, booting him about like a sack of spuds. Tony said, 'Shall we help him?'

'You must be joking, mate.'

We couldn't do anything. We stayed on the train and ended up in Wakefield. We didn't get home until about 3am.

Leeds's formidable reputation eventually made them a prime target for the police and in the late eighties dozens of them were arrested in a big swoop. Some were jailed in June, 1988, four months after the Guvnors were lifted. But they continued to do the business. They're great wreckers. In 1990 they caused £20,000–worth of damage to seats at Maine Road, tried to pull down the perimeter fencing and wrecked gates. Our is one rivalry that the Old Bill can never quash.

# 7

## *On The Town*

MY fighting exploits weren't confined to the football terraces. I started going out regularly in 'town' – Manchester city centre – in my teens. It was a strange environment for my mates and I because you didn't see many black guys in town in the 1970s. They stuck to Moss Side, to their own pubs and clubs like the Nile, the Reno, the reggae scene. That wasn't for me; I wasn't interested in the music, for a start. We were one of the first cliques of black and half-caste lads to go into town regularly.

We had untold problems. I never came home at a weekend without blood on my shirt. I used to drive my mam mad; she started comfort-eating and put on weight. The fights didn't seem as bad as they are now; you weren't getting potted with a glass or stabbed. You'd have a bit of a battle, then it would be over and the next week you could go in the same pub. I knew when we went out that it would kick off and if it did I could rely on my mates. We played football together, watched football together and went out at night together. Thursday, Friday, Saturday, Sunday, I was with the same people.

We were a mixed group, white, black and half-caste. We all drank lager, going in pubs from the age of sixteen, places like Genevieve's, Cloisters, Placemates 7, the Piccadily Club, Brewsters, the John Bull Bar. Cloisters had a 50p-a-drink night. It was mainly a United hangout and was the first place in town to have plastic glasses because the real ones kept getting smashed. Then there was the Victoria Bar, off Deansgate. Every drink in there was 50p until 10pm. We would meet there at 7.30pm, get tanked up for less than a fiver, then pay 50p to get in Cloisters. Later we moved to the Cyprus Tavern on Princess Street, and the Cellar Vie, which was also a United bar originally but was eventually taken over by City. United fans often drank in Shambles Square and around St Anne's Square. That was their patch. City fans could usually be found more on the edges of the centre.

Though I was always out, I have never been a heavy drinker. Some of the lads were known as the Beer Monsters and they really could drink. They always wanted to stay in the pub until kick-off time. We had lots of them, lads like Bulldog, Big Kevin, Scotty and all the older boys. When we were teenagers we wanted to be out hunting around but they were the main boys then and they'd just drink the beer, get pissed, sing songs, miss all the action and go and watch the match.

By now I was working and had the money to go to the football and go out at night. One of my best mates, Bob Green, a bit of a hard lad from Eccles, worked for a firm in Monton called Altitude Scaffolding. He kept telling me I should try for a job there. The only way you could get the job was if you had transport. I was to be his 'joey', or labourer, picking him up and taking him round. So I bought a Vauxhall Viva for £25 and said, 'Right Bob, I've got a car now, get me a job.'

Bob went to the two bosses of the firm and said, 'I've got a new lad for you, he's called Mickey, er . . . he's me cousin.'

So the bosses said, 'Bring him down.'

I went to the yard pretending to be his cousin. Bob's white, with blond hair, I'm brown with a big curly afro.

The bloke in charge, obviously an observant sort, says, 'You're not his cousin.'

'I am.'

'Don't take the piss. Can you read and write?'

'Course I can read and write.'

'Right, you can start.'

So there I was, a scaffolder's labourer. I loved that job, and stayed with them for five or six years until the company changed hands.

It was hard for any young man to find work at that time, but it was twice as difficult if you were black. It didn't make things easier with me having no qualifications, and being the way I was, not taking any shit from anyone. Even the scaffolding company got a bit worried about me in the end because of the way I put myself over.

One day, when I was twenty-two, they said, 'Mike, go to New Mills to do a job.'

New Mills is miles away in Derbyshire. We were paid £4 travel money a day in our wages, maximum. I was pretty sure that wouldn't get me there and back. I got as far as Alderley Edge, in Cheshire, before the car chugged to a stop.

I was fuming. I rang the firm and said, 'I'm going to come down there and give you what's what.' Or words to that effect.

'Look, Mickey, you might as well go home, forget the job.'

I had to buy some more petrol myself to get home. The next morning, I went in the yard to get my next job and to have a word with them. They said there was no work that day and told me to go home again. I got halfway home and snapped. I thought, cheeky bastards, I've got out of bed and they're sending me home. I drove back to the yard where the other lads were waiting to go to work and jumped out of the car like a madman. I kicked the office door and shouted, 'I'm not fucking going home, I want a fucking day's work for a fucking day's pay. I got out of fucking bed, you find me somewhere local to work.'

And they gave me a nice local job. I thought, I've got these over a barrel here. But they liked me because I was a bit of character. People who didn't know me very well didn't always take to me because I did some naughty stuff. People that had sussed me out knew I was a cunt and usually enjoyed my company. I did things off instinct and thought later. I didn't know any better. I got myself in some right problems. There have been situations where I could have been killed, not just at football but later on when I worked as a nightclub bouncer, but somehow I have always walked away from them.

One rather big incident that thankfully I didn't get involved in was the Moss Side rioting in July, 1981. The main problems were on Princess Road, only a five-minute walk from Acomb Street, but I stayed out of it. It was bad. For two nights, more than 1,000 youths ransacked shops, threw petrol bombs and set fire to cars and buildings. They even besieged Moss Side police station.

Despite that, I reckon the cops had it boxed off. They moved out of the immediate area a bit and let the worst of it blow over. A lot of people said the spark was police harassment but I think it was just a copycat thing. You had the Brixton riots, Toxteth, Leeds, Bristol, everyone jumping on the bandwagon. They were all black areas, supposedly depressed areas, and they all kicked off.

Some of our lads got roped in. The worst to suffer was Jimmy Gittings. He was only seventeen and already had a conviction for football hooliganism but on this occasion he was standing at a bus stop, minding his own business, when the police lifted him. He was charged with throwing a petrol bomb, causing an affray and 'possessing articles with intent to damage uniforms and riot shields.' The police said he was part of a mob that attacked a post office. Jimmy always denied it and there was uproar when he was found guilty and jailed for six years at Manchester Crown Court a few months later. His sentence was cut to four years on appeal.

Another of the City lads to cop it was Donald Farrer. He was done for helping to start a fire which caused £110,000–worth of damage to a hardware shop in Princess Road. He apparently told the police, 'Someone got a bomb and threw it. I could see it was not alight properly, so I got one and threw it towards the back of the shop.' That's Donald for you. His defence counsel said, 'He is like many black youths with no job and no future. His future is even more bleak because of his lack of skills.' The judge was quite lenient and sent him to borstal, even though he was twenty.

Police harassment was a fact in Moss Side. Now you don't know who the coppers are, they are that discreet, with surveillance cameras and stakeouts. When I was young, the Old Bill would give you a belt and that would be it. Now they have to go by the book. I'm sure they are scared of Moss Side. They say there are no no-go

Me today: a football hooligan no longer.

*Top:* City fan Hamrick Bryan being helped from Maine Road with a dart in his head during a derby game against United in the 70s. *Above left:* City club steward Ken Smith after he was battered by Leeds fans at Elland Road while trying to protect his seven year old son.

*Centre right and above:* Wetherby's in Port Street in the city centre after a mass battle between City and man United in February 1990.

Donald Farrer: saw a psychiatrist to treat his compulsion to attend football matches.

My brother Chris, pictured outside Liverpool Crown Court during the Guvnors trial in 1989.

*Above:* Me and Mark Dorrian talking outside court. *Below:* Some 'calling cards' which City hooligan gangs carried to be left at the scenes of their crimes.

just been done

M.
B.
M.

With Compliments

FROM THE
**MANCHESTER CITY**
MAYNE-LINE
**BEER MONSTERS**

YOU'VE JUST B

**MCF**

MAINLINE MOTORWAY SERVICE

YOU'VE JUST BEEN TUNED IN BY THE

**MCFC**

EW

The business has just been done
by the

**M.C.F.C.**

Mini Bus Mafia

M.
B.
M.

Business as usual

Congratulations

**YOU'VE JUST MET**
**THE BOARD OF THE**
**YOUNG GUVNORS**

David Foulkes

David Goodhall

Mark Fiorini

Andrew Bennion

James Gittings

Paul Derry

Anthony Worthington

Mark Dorrian

James Roberts

A gallery of Guvnors. Pictures taken outside Liverpool Crown Court during our trial in 1989. All of the lads pictured pleaded guilty.

areas but there are. Salford is a no-go area at certain times, so is Cheetham Hill, so is Moss Side. It's very rare you see a copper on the beat in Moss Side. You show me one and I'll show my arse.

After the riots, a former Lord Mayor of Manchester gave her view of Moss Side in a report. It gives an idea of what the area was like at that time. She said, 'The tragedy of Moss Side hung in the atmosphere after the worst affrays of July had ceased – a silence, a fear, nobody wanting to speak of the two nights. The damage done to trade, to shops in the area concerned, to restaurants, to leisure and entertainment facilities, is enormous, perhaps never to be recovered. People who daily pass through the area do not stop – indeed it is possibly unfortunate that the main route into the city from affluent Cheshire passes through Moss Side. Women alone stay firmly at home after dark and refuse to open their locked and barred doors.'

Mind you, I wouldn't like to walk on my own through Moss Side now. As you get older you realise how dangerous things are. You have no fear when you are younger but as you get older, you see how things have changed, you hear of people getting kicked to death for fuck all. If I leave a club, I get a taxi or get driven home. I don't like walking anywhere on my own. I suppose it's because I've seen so much trouble. How many times do you read about people getting kicked into comas? Too many. Who wants to be a victim?

★ ★ ★

I left home when I was nineteen to live with my then-girlfriend, Leoni Gregory, in Gladeside Road, Wythenshawe, next to the Silver Birch pub. We had a daughter, called Keeley. She's eighteen now. We also had an alsatian called Zimba. I soon got to know people in the area. It was pretty rough but not as bad as Moss Side, nothing I couldn't handle. People knew who I was, I was pretty well known and made friends easily but the move didn't really work out. It took me away from a lot of things I was doing. I wanted to be in the thick of it all.

Eventually I moved back to Moss Side, to stay on the Alexandra Park estate with my uncle. That was a bit of an experience. Even in that period, Moss Side had changed. Alex Park, a kind of oasis of low-rise council housing set back off Princess Road, is weird. It was a throwback to my childhood; everyone was out and about but it had become very gang-oriented. Years later, it was the scene for a gang feud that left a lot of bodies in the streets and earned Manchester the nickname 'Gunchester.' I never mixed in those circles. I left in the morning to work as a scaffolder, came home, ate my tea and got out. I knew the main lads, they knew me, but I never got involved with them.

If you had an argument when I was a kid, it often led to a fight, but they took it a step further. It became all guns and drugs. Whereas we used to ride our bikes and do nothing worse than nick the odd car, now they're all cruising in GTis and carrying mobile phones, just kids. They're in a big, vicious circle.

\* \* \*

While I was preoccupied with violence, both on and off the terraces, there were actually some football matches going on. In 1977 and 1978, City finished second and then fourth in the League. After that, they hovered around mid-table for several seasons. We also started playing managerial musical chairs. Mercer and Allison went, then Allison came back, then he went again, to be replaced by John Bond. In 1981, despite another average season in the League, we had an unexpected run in the FA Cup. On April 11, I had the best twenty-first birthday present anyone could want when we played Ipswich in the semi-final at Villa Park. By now I had got rid of my Vauxhall Viva and bought a red Escort Popular. I put a Man City flag on the front, scarves sticking out of the windows, and we set off early in the morning, all in cars. In my car was Bob Green, Dave Israel, who we called Izzy, and his older brother, a big bastard who used to knock us all about; he smacked our heads together once and nearly knocked us out. There were thousands of City fans on the M6, leaning out of windows, honking their horns, swigging out of cans.

As usual, there was a bit of trouble, although for once I wasn't involved. Some of the City NF lot went round Paki-bashing and attacking Asian shops. We just had a really good day. There were a few Ipswich fans in the bottom of the stand and they got wasted but nothing major. The match was great. City won 1–0, Paul Power scoring from a free kick, top corner, and we were on our way to Wembley. A birthday party had been arranged for me at my house that night with my girlfriend and all my family. I never turned up. I stayed in Birmingham getting pissed with the City fans while everyone was sitting at the house waiting. There were no mobile phones then, so they couldn't mither me. We drove back very slowly, taking it all in, and on the way we saw the Man United team coach. They had been playing Coventry. We were screaming out of the windows at them.

So we were in an FA Cup Final, against Spurs. I didn't go. I had a ticket, Donald arranged the coach, and after all that, I got up late and missed it. I watched the final in our house with my mam, with two cans of lager. I was gutted. Donald was pissed off because they had waited to pick me up in Wythenshawe and I hadn't turned up. So I sat on the couch with my ticket in my hand. City, of course, drew 1–1 but lost in the replay when Ricky Villa scored that raggy goal. I never went to that, either.

In the 1982–3 season, City finished tenth in the League. It was dominated by Liverpool, who thrashed us 5–0 at Anfield. But worse was to come. The 1983–4 season started well and after thirteen games we were in second place. Then it all went wrong. In the second half of the season we won four out of twenty matches. That left us with Luton at home on the last day, May 14, to stay up.

Hundreds of us met up in the Parkside. We were all drinking heavily and all pissing about. Inside the ground, I pulled a faint, just for the buzz. The lads passed me down the ground and the police had to carry me out. One of them was saying, 'Ah, he's fucking about. We'll take him through the Luton end.'

I think they were expecting me to jump up and say, 'No thanks.'

But I kept still and eventually they carried me behind the Kippax into a first aid room. The City team doctor was brought in and told them I had either suffered an epileptic fit or was a glue sniffer!

Bob Green had come with me but told the police, 'I don't know him, I was just standing next to him when he caved over.'

I decided to kick off in the medical room and grabbed Bob by the face. He yelped and shouted, 'Mickey, no, it's me, let go.'

Then I grabbed a copper by the face, ripping his nose and his ears, pretending I was having a fit. I broke off the bed and chased this ancient steward down a corridor. Then all these screws held me down and someone gave me an injection. An ambulance came and took me to Manchester Royal Infirmary.

When I got there, someone told me the match result. Nil-one to Luton. We were down. They put me in a room with police standing outside. This big black woman came in, a cleaner, and Bob said to her, 'These police are out of order, they keep banging him because he's black.'

'No, you're joking, aren't you? He's done nothing wrong.'

She went outside to give the coppers a piece of her mind. I grabbed my Dr Marten boots, lobbed them through the window, jumped out and legged it. When I arrived home, two coppers were standing outside the door.

'How have you got out?' one of them asked.

'They let me go.'

I went in the house and that was it. Nothing more said. But for the next two days I couldn't get out of bed because of the injection they gave me. I was blinded. So I missed our relegation but on the whole I had a great day.

# 8

## *The Mayne Line*

BEING in Division Two for the first time in seventeen years was a blow to the club but a boost to us hooligans. City's crowds stayed up – over 25,000 on average at home – and we were playing a lot of teams relatively near to Manchester: Bradford City, Blackburn Rovers, Oldham Athletic, Huddersfield Town, Sheffield Wednesday. The Second Division at that time also had some of the top mobs in the country: Leeds, Chelsea, Newcastle, Middlesbrough, Cardiff City and Portsmouth. We stayed down there for two seasons and had riots.

The Cool Cats were fizzling out. A lot of the older guys lost interest. By 1983, all over the country, the old hands from the rampaging days were giving way to new mobs: the casuals. Football fashion, which started subtly at first, was in full swing, partly as a method of fooling the Bill, who were still on the lookout for the snarling skinhead with his scarves and bovver boots and tended to overlook the smartly dressed young chaps sitting in the first-class carriage or the executive coach. The styles had regional variations – I remember playing Notts Forest and they were all wearing green flight jackets – but mostly the look was similar: straight jeans, expensive trainers, woollen golfing pullies, loads of labels. The Scousers, who probably started it all, were dead trendy. So were the Cockneys. In Manchester, Kappa stuff was big. My trademark was a blue Nike baseball cap. I wore it everywhere for about five seasons. I always wore leather gloves as well; not for fashion but to protect my hands.

A lot of the new casual firms took their names from the scheduled train services they used to avoid the heavily-policed football specials: West Ham's Inter-City Firm, the Leeds Service Crew, Liverpool's Ordinary Mob (the 'ordinary' was Scouse slang for the service train – Scousers have to be different), Porstsmouth's 6.57 Crew. Our preferred method of transport was the coach: it was cheap and you could set off when you wanted, stop where you wanted and leave when you wanted. Donald did all our hiring and regularly used a firm called Mayne Line in Clayton, Manchester. I don't think they ever realised what we were up to. It became our habit to stop at motorway service stations on the way to and from matches to look for rival fans and so we became known as the Mayne Line Motorway Service Crew. It was a gradual change; some people still called us the Cool Cats years later.

Donald set up a travel club, with membership dues entitling you to reduced rate fares on the coach. We took crates of beer on board. The drivers didn't care, they knew we were all mad and anyway they got a nice whip-round at the end of the journey. Donald had a strict set of rules and had flyers printed with the disclaimer, 'Anybody who travels on a Mayne Line coach does so at their own risk.' We also printed calling cards with the message, 'You've just been tuned in by the M.C.F.C. Mayne Line Motorway Service Crew.'

I was pretty confident of my fighting abilities by now. I liked to pick people out as targets, usually the gobby ones who did all the shouting, 'Come on!' and all that. But normally you don't get a chance to pick somebody out because when it kicks off you just rush in. The fights rarely last long. There might be a bit of a build up, a lot of running and shouting, but the actual contact isn't great. You could run a mob of 100 lads and only four or five might get caught and weighed in. The rest get away or get a quick smack.

I never worried about the size of someone. The bigger, the better. There were plenty who'd shout, 'Get the big feller. Get him first.' It's a way of frightening the opposition. They think that if you go straight for their top lads, you must be a handful. I was confident I could handle myself because I've always had to. Where I was brought up, if you didn't look after yourself you got walked on.

I can take a punch. I've been punched many times, so I know. I've been in one-on-ones and never been done over. I've been weighed in and I've come through it. If you want to go and do something, you've got to be able to take it as well. I've been in pubs with fifty lads and we've been rushed by 150–200 and you had to fight your way out of it or get fucking hammered, there was no choice.

We would stop at every service station en route to a game and anyone who was there got a taste. We also 'taxed' the service stations. They used to get ravaged. Whole shelves of cakes and biscuits would disappear. You'd get on the coach and everyone's jaw would be munching. We had a guy called Bulldog who was very fat and always eating. Once we stopped at a service station on the way to London and steamed the restaurant. Bulldog grabbed this bloke's plate of eggs and chips off his tray and poured it into his coat pocket. When we got back on the coach he sat there and ate the egg and chips with his hands from out of his pocket. No matter who we played, he always came back with a black eye, or battered. He wouldn't take his City scarf off anywhere, he was never alert, and if it kicked off he was too fat to get away. He was a typical football fan, always a pie in one hand and a pint of beer in the other.

There were some real characters. Kippax Debbie was a girl who ran with the Gorton Blues. She could fight. She was built like a bloke and I have seen her get stuck in like a bloke. She had fair hair and she wore all the gear, scarves on her wrist and belt and head and Doc Marten boots. You wouldn't necessarily have wanted her as your girlfriend but she was a loyal City fan, loved the Blues and used to egg the lads on, 'Come on, let's have the bastards.' Dead game. I don't know what happened to her but I heard a story that she threw herself under a train in Longsight.

Then there were the jibbers, the scroungers, like Charlie Sow. He would turn up with no cash and go round the train or coach with his hand out, 'Have you got 10p, lend us 10p mate.' He'd collect his money, get enough for a beer, watch the match, scrounge again for his fare home and come back with more money than he'd gone with. He's a good lad, Charlie. He works the club doors now. Probably still jibbing off the customers.

Donald was the boss. He banned scarves and banners and enforced smart dress only. Anyone who damaged one of the coaches was dealt with the Francis way. He battered Charlie Sow once after an argument, chased him round Maine Road, grabbed him and filled him in against a wall outside. Charlie likes to tell the story. He says, 'Donald was kicking me that much, in the end he only stopped because he was tired.' Donald ruled the roost a bit when he was younger.

When it kicked off, the same faces were always there. We had one firm who came up from Bristol in a minibus for every game. Sometimes they filled a coach and they were a right bunch of yobs, the Bristol Blues. They had a good reputation. All the way from Bristol to watch City play. They must have been mad.

Donald always says that the Mayne Line were headline grabbers and, compared to the Cool Cats, they were. One of the first incidents in which they were involved, and one which made it big in the papers and on TV, was our trip to Blackpool for the third round of the FA Cup in January, 1984. I don't much like Blackpool but all the lads loved it and wanted to go there early and have a drink. We actually went on the train, getting there for about 10.30am, and went to the Manchester Arms, a big pub on the South Promenade which is a popular spot for visiting Mancs.

Someone said there was a mob of Blackpool in another pub so we went looking and found three of them – that was it. But in the end they did turn out. Tickets had been really hard to come by and we went down to the ground to see if we could find any spares for the lads. One scam we had was to send someone into the ticket office to ask if a ticket had been reserved for Mr Smith. The sales girl would look through the pile of reserves and the lad would make a mental note of a couple of names by reading them upside down. Of course, there was no Mr Smith. He would then walk out, give the names he had just read to someone else, they would go in and claim the tickets, spotting a couple more names themselves, then repeat the procedure until everyone was sorted.

We didn't bother with that at Bloomfield Road. We just steamed the ticket office and snatched a pile. As we came out, a good little firm of about thirty Seasiders turned up. They steamed straight in and gave us a run for our money until more City arrived and we saw them off. Incidentally, the demand for tickets had been so great that some of the lads were later done for trying to sell forgeries outside the ground.

A young City mob, the Young Guvnors, was also starting to surface at this time. This is how one of them remembered the Blackpool trip in a newspaper interview:

It was just unbelievable that day. Our lads took liberties all day long. They robbed the club ticket office before the match and were selling the tickets outside to City fans, so a lot of the City supporters got into the Blackpool end. Our lads had just charged into the ticket office – the tickets were just lying out in open view on the side – and snatched them up. It was able to happen because at low division clubs like Blackpool neither the club nor the coppers know the score and have not had much experience of handling big crowds.

When Blackpool scored their goals, all hell broke loose. The City fans turned on the police and started fighting them and the police backed off. A couple of Manchester lads had got on to the roof of the stand and were chucking the asbestos off. Chunks of it were falling down and our lads started throwing it at the police. That was going on for about forty minutes and the police couldn't control it. Then they drafted in reinforcements from Merseyside and they came in real strong with truncheons.

The City fans ran out on to the pitch and the police brought in dogs to move them but they refused to move. The game was held up. Finally the cops forced our lads back into the visiting supporters' end but the fans were trying to get at the police for the rest of the match.

We lost the game 2–1. Afterwards we went on the beach, all jumping in the water. We stayed in Blackpool until about 10pm and got barred from all the pubs. They had bouncers on every door and we had more trouble with them than anyone else. We ended up getting bottles from off licences and singing on the promenade but the police weren't having it, they charged us three or four times, and more or less forced us to the station and escorted us out of Blackpool. Some lads stayed down for the weekend.

The trouble inside the ground at Blackpool was repeated when we played Oldham on what became known as Bad Good Friday, April 20, 1984. It was day of total anarchy. According to the *Oldham Chronicle*, 'Gangs of marauding soccer fans brought violence and terror to the streets of Oldham and Chadderton. Windows were smashed, shops and pubs robbed, motorists stopped, assaulted and robbed.' More than £600 in turnstile takings was stolen from the ground and a programme seller was mugged.

Inside Boundary Park, City fans in the Rochdale Road End climbed over the security fence and invaded the pitch. We stormed the Ford Stand paddock and then climbed up into the stand. There were only two coppers there and they were helpless. Once in the stand, the lads took complete control, preventing the Athletic fans who had paid for their tickets from taking their seats. A lot of them were so scared they just turned round and went home. The fighting spread to the Chadderton Road end, normally reserved for home fans.

More dibble arrived and four of them were hurt in the melee, one of them a sergeant felled by a piece of concrete hurled from the stands. The game was held up while police, club officials and the referee decided what to do. The Oldham chairman Ian Stott later said, 'In the end, we had to leave the stand to the invading fans. If we had tried to get them out, all hell might have broken loose.' Thirty-seven fans were arrested for public order offences at the ground and eventually 100 were ejected.

We didn't always have things our own way. The next month we played Chelsea at home and faced a truly massive mob who came to see their club promoted. We got a taste of our own medicine that night (see Chapter Ten). But the trouble at the ground wasn't the end of it. A van load of Chelsea stopped off on their way home at a pub in Chesterfield. A gang of locals, including some City fans, got into them and eighteen people ended up being done for affray for what the court called 'a most disgraceful exhibition of violence.'

Knives were appearing more and more at matches. I never held with them but every mob had its knifers and I can't say that we were an exception. This report is from the Wolverhampton *Express and Star* about a match at the start of the next season, on September 4:

Two Wolverhampton men suffered horrific injuries

after a gang of knife-wielding Manchester football thugs went on the rampage.

They left one man with blood pouring from an eight-inch wound after slashing him with a Stanley knife. And another youth needed 30 stitches in a wound stretching from his ear to his jaw.

The thugs had been among 2,000 Manchester City fans who saw their side lose 2–0 at Molineux last night.

The trouble had been brewing at the ground. This is from solicitor's notes for the case of a City lad who was nicked, who I shall call JS:

At some stage, about 150 people ran down the terraces towards the fence separating the terrace from the pitch. Once over that fence, had they crossed it, it would have given them access to Molineux stand. A short time before, there had been a rumpus between the visitors and the home supporters in Molineux stand.

The police officers moved forward to stop people crossing over the fence in front of the visitors' stand. It is alleged that JS was part of the group of 150. One officer indeed pushed JS away from the fence, the officer then turned away, heard JS say, 'Fucking bastards,' and JS pushed back towards the fence. He also encouraged the others to do the same. The officer heard him say this, the others there were not so noisy that they could not distingush what JS was saying, therefore they moved in to arrest him.

He was initially taken to the police room below Molineux stand, where he was searched and found to be in possession of fifty small, green cards, with, 'You've just been tuned in by MCFC Mayne Line Motorway Service Crew' on them. The officer in the case understands that 'tuned' means beaten or thumped. Prosecution's solicitor mentioned that there is a gang going round the Wolverhampton area that leave cards on their victims, saying word to the effect that you have just been cut up by whatever the gang is. The police are clearly suggesting to the magistrates that the cards found on JS have a similar meaning. It is clearly open to interpretation.

Sergeant Box at Red Line Police Station, near the ground, merely charges the defendant, who, however, says in reply to the charge, 'Sorry.'

A month later, we played Blackpool again in the Milk Cup. They spent £15,000 putting up new security fencing, a police observation post and an anti-missile net to prevent a repeat of the January episode. There were twenty-four arrests but nothing more serious than a few fireworks going off and someone throwing an egg at City's manager, Billy McNeill.

Probably our most notorious battle in the Mayne Line days was at Rothersthorpe service station, on the M1 near Northampton, on December 15, 1984. We were returning from a game at Charlton and should have stopped at Watford Gap but it was full. We pulled up at Rothersthorpe, three coachloads of City, all the boys, and saw about eight coaches of Stoke City fans. They had played Chelsea. The service station security staff had deliberately made our coaches park at opposite ends of the service station but it didn't work.

The Stoke fans had gone through a glass-partitioned

bridge onto the other side to get some food. Two of our lads went over and came back with their noses busted. So we went up and it kicked off near the toilets. A huge, running fight went on for the next eight minutes. They ran us one way, we ran them back. They smashed up one of our coaches, we wrecked one of theirs. Fighting spilled over the entire service station. The food court looked like a warzone. Even blokes with their wives were getting involved. The cops only managed to separate us by driving a car between the two groups. Forty-four of our lot were nicked and all fifty-six Stoke fans from one coach. They kept the lads in for about nine hours before releasing them. Their coach was so badly damaged that it had to be taken out of service.

A police spokesman told the Press, 'All the windows along one side of the Stoke coach were smashed. The behaviour of the fans brought no credit to their clubs. After being interviewed at the police stations, the supporters were given a police escort out of the county.'

Some of the lads were in cars and I jumped in with them because I knew it would come on top for those on the coach. I thought, I'll see you in Manchester, I've had my day out. Afterwards we had to pay the coach company for the windows. That wasn't a problem. The coaches were shit, proper old wrecks. They were happy because we were ordering three coaches a fortnight, every fortnight.

I got away, but Donald ended up in hospital – and later in prison:

*The whole lot went up. We put about twelve of their people in hospital. But they put a fire extinguisher on my chest and smashed my ribs in. They had a right go back. I was*

*taken to Northampton General from where I did a runner
and got caught again at Rugby railway station. I was in
agony. I eventually got six months in jail.*

*I went down for breakfast one morning with my metal
tray. This big black guy next to me spat in my breakfast.
Then another one spat in it, then another one rubbed the
end of his dick with his hand, then smeared his hand on
my toast and said, 'There's your cheese on toast.'*

*This geezer could have eaten me alive but I whacked
him with the tray, jumped on him and was biting him and
everything. I got a bit of respect after that because everyone
thought I was a nutter.*

*When I got the sentence at Stoke, I went to a prison
near Nottingham. I was on the block for two weeks because
all the other guys were going to kill me but I ended up
studying for a business degree and was captain of the
football team. One of the prison officers looked out for me.
In fact I have never had a hard time off screws. I was the
only Manc in there but I got respect. It was like a barracks.*

*What made me do it was the adrenalin rush, the buzz.
You get on a coach with fifty lads, go 200 miles away and
have a fucking good ruck. It is like sex but it lasts longer.*

In January, 1985, we were knocked out of the FA Cup
at Coventry City. So we ripped out the seats and threw
them on to the pitch. In total, 500 seats were damaged
and four stewards were attacked when they tried to stop
us getting on to the pitch. In March, it went off at
Birmingham in a night match. Hundreds of their fans
invaded the pitch at the end and were chased off by
mounted police. A City fan was stabbed after the game
near New Street station and one of his mates had to
climb up some scaffolding to get away. In April, we

smashed up a dozen buses taking Leeds fans back to Victoria Station after a game at Maine Road.

Despite all these off-field distractions, the team had actually got its act together on the pitch and, with two games to go, we were on the brink of promotion. Thousands travelled to Notts County, who were up near the top as well, for a crunch game on May 6. By half-time, we were 3–0 down. Fighting started in the stands and the mounted police were brought in when people started ripping up fences. The game was held up for half an hour. When it finally ended, forty fans invaded the City dressing room. We ended up losing 3–2 but thrashed Charlton 5–1 in our last home game and were promoted in third place. Now we were back with the big boys.

\* \* \*

Events elsewhere were finally to lead to a concerted effort to rid British football of hooliganism. The Millwall riot at Luton in March, 1985, the death of a fan at the Birmingham City-Leeds game and, above all, the Heysel Stadium tragedy in Brussels, caused the banning of English clubs from European competition and brought about a new mood of determination on behalf of the authorities to crack down on people like me. Margaret Thatcher took a personal interest and even set up a 'war cabinet' to tackle the problem. The new anti-hooligan mood reached everywhere. In June 1985, during the close season, the local paper reported:

Manchester City has been forced to close down the Platt Lane stand to its own supporters at the insistence of police. The tough new security measures, following last season's problems, mean – in City's case – that the entire Platt Lane stand will now be reserved for visiting fans.

Blues supporters who have already bought season tickets for Platt Lane will now be offered more expensive seats in the North Stand at no extra cost. And the club are urging any such season ticket holders to contact the main ticket office without delay.

Says City secretary Bernard Halford, 'We are sorry that any of our Platt Lane regulars will be inconvenienced but we do understand why the police have insisted on this measure. The measures being taken are in the interest of safety for everybody in the ground . . . both home fans and visiting fans.'

It was safety outside the ground that was the problem. We had pubs like the Parkside, the Sherwood Inn and others around the area that were ideal bases to organise from. On match days, we'd be out early, hunting around, or 'scalping,' sussing out who was parking where and who was about. We'd get spotters out, younger lads, who would look at car registrations, window stickers, scarves on back seats and other signs of where someone was from. If there were four or five cars from out of town they'd get done straight away or you'd wait to ambush them after the match. We were nearly all local lads and it was easy for us to spot an outsider.

But the Bill were getting better at their job – slowly. The old days, when you could rampage without worrying, were passing and because sentences were getting heavier, we would go to greater measures to rescue lads from arrest.

September, 1985. The new season is barely a month old and the Mayne Line Service Crew has struck again:

A mob of Manchester City fans swept through a motorway service area late last night on an orgy of looting. The rampaging coachload – on their way home after the Blues' 1–0 defeat at Birmingham – created fear and panic at Sandbach on the M6 in Cheshire.

The thugs caught services management by surprise after parking their coach in a corner of the northbound car park. They then crossed the motorway bridge and ran riot on the other side.

Thirty hooligans burst into the gift shop, sweeping aside manageress Mrs Patricia Riley and helping themselves to armfuls of cigarettes, sweets and cassette tapes. Mrs Riley raised the alarm and the mob was tackled by two detectives who were having a cup of tea in the cafe nearby.

The thugs fled, dropping some of their loot, and terrorised diners in the restaurant before they escaped. Two men were arrested and one was due to appear in court at Sandbach on alleged theft and offensive weapon charges.

Mr Barry Aldridge, shopping manager for Rochdale Services, said today: 'They stole about £80–worth of cigarettes. They simply rushed into the shop, pushed the girl to one side and helped themselves to as much as they could before getting out. We are getting used to this kind of thing – we were looted three times last season. These people are not interested in football, they are only interested in what they can get out of trouble and violence.'

Donald Farrer was one of the lads who was arrested, as usual. The two detectives put him in a police car which was then surrounded by a mob of City who rocked it and tried to get him out. The cops managed to get him away to Congleton police station where they searched him and found a Stanley knife and two tile cutters in his pockets. He was jailed for ninety days after admitting stealing eighty fags but was cleared of an offensive weapons charge. The dibble claimed in court that in a statement he said, 'I got my knife because they are good on people's faces. I was going to use them to get the Brummies.' Donald denied ever saying it and the magistrates came down in his favour.

We could find trouble anywhere. It didn't have to be at a soccer ground or a service station. We played at Nottingham Forest shortly after and our coach dropped us off next to some playing fields. A few amateur teams were playing rugby on the pitches.

One of the lads said, 'Let's do the rugby players.'

Someone else, half joking, said, 'Fuck off, they're mad, they'll do us in.'

But once it had been said, we had to do it. So we ran onto the field and steamed into these rugby players. All the other teams saw what was happening, stopped playing and came running over to help them and we had a huge battle with these maniacs in their shorts and boots. Those rugby boys really wanted to know and in the end we retreated, laughing our socks off. The day ended badly for me when I was arrested for an attack on a petrol station, but that's another story (see Chapter Nine).

For our Donald, there was to be one more arrest and that was it. Towards the end of the 1985–6 season, we played Newcastle away:

*My last sentence was against Newcastle. They have got a very good, tasty firm. It is a rough area, they haven't got a lot going for them. We parked the coaches and didn't have to wait long before they found us on the Haymarket. They came at us like a bat out of hell. We ran into the bus station and everyone had to do the business.*

*For some reason we had a mob within a mob that day, Foster and about fifteen other black guys. All of a sudden they came to the front and the Geordies panicked. They hadn't seen a black mob before. Then Mike and everyone joined in. The Geordies couldn't handle it. We walked to the ground and they wouldn't come near us. So I had all the white guys on the inside and all the black guys on the outside. Even the coppers wouldn't come near us. Up there there are no black people.*

*I was in the middle, planning with the squad. We had snatch squads going out. When we came out after the game, they really had a tasty firm because we had taken liberties. We went into their Arndale Centre and ran amok. We did 'duranies' where you bang the till in a shop and it opens and you take the money. Others were doing jewellery shops. It kicked off with the shopping centre security and we did them and threw them down escalators. The police pinpointed me and came in for me but the lads backed me up and it took about thirty of them to get me.*

*Gradually I was getting business-minded. When the bus drivers refused to run to matches in Manchester, I hired buses from Burnley and Pendle Transport. I eventually got the contract for the buses taking away supporters from the special at Piccadilly train station to the ground. I was a lot happier making money than sitting in jail.*

*Nearly all of my convictions are for public order offences. I have never stolen in my life. I have been done for drunk and disorderly and I don't even drink. I'm squeaky-clean now. I would never go to a football match again. They would have to pay me.*

# 9

## Nicked and Battered

THE worst sight in the world is a charge sheet. We spent a lot of time trying to avoid arrest but any serious soccer hooligan knows that, sooner or later, it's going to happen. I have been nicked at football about ten times, at places as far apart as Manchester, Leeds, Middlesbrough, Nottingham, Shrewsbury, Arsenal, Newcastle and West Ham. At Maine Road, the police knew me by name. If ever there was trouble and I was in the area, they knew I had been involved. But they could never catch me doing anything. I outwitted them for a long time, until they got the spy cameras in, because I knew the set up at Maine Road so well. Still, how we got away with some stuff was unbelievable.

My first arrest at an away match was for throwing missiles at Derby County's Baseball Ground. I was in my mid-teens. Their fans were chucking stuff into our section of the ground. I had a Coke bottle with me, so I lobbed it over at them. Two coppers picked me out and I was arrested. They locked me in one of the police horse boxes and eventually took me to the nick, booked me and let me go at about 6.30pm. Of course, I had to make my own way home. I was back in court the following month, pleaded guilty and got a small fine. About twenty City fans were there with me; I hadn't realised anyone else had been arrested because we had been kept in separate cells. It's often the case these days that they lock you up for the weekend and you all appear together in court on Monday morning.

There were occasions, however, where the dibble did you a favour by lifting you. In one of our forays to Leeds, I was arrested for breaking the segregation area inside the ground. I jumped over the barrier and ran at the Leeds fans on my own. Fortunately, I didn't reach them. I was grabbed by the police before the Leeds could get me, which was just as well, because they would have killed me. As it was, I got a hiding off the police and was carried out, legs in the air, arms up my back. The lads were loving it. I could hear them all singing, 'Goodbye, Mickey, goodbye. We'll see you again, we don't know when. Goodbye, Mickey, goodbye.' I was fined £80.

I was saved by the bizzies again at Newcastle, this time in a Cup game. It was one of the most frightening days of my life. We were escorted to the ground and inside were put in a pen, 3,000 of us, surrounded by a sea of black and white. Newcastle's firm invaded our end; the police let the fuckers in. These big spud-eaters pinned us in a corner and I was nicked, fighting for my life. I was dragged out again, locked up for the weekend and in court on the Monday. When I got back to Manchester, I found out that everyone that went with me had been absolutely hammered. They had lumps on their heads and I was unmarked. The police had apparently taken the City out at the end, put them in what looked like a cattle market and locked them in for an hour to let the Newcastle disperse. But when they were finally let out, Newcastle were still waiting in their thousands. They're crazy up there. City got bombarded from everywhere and chased all round the town.

All of those north-east clubs have firms. Middlesbrough is just as bad. I went up there for the League Cup semi-final on January 10, 1976, the year City played Newcastle in the final. I was fifteen. They beat us 1–0 at their ground. Coaches always got smashed up there so we went in four transit vans, twenty lads in each. We left the vans in a car park and went for a look around. We couldn't understand a word anyone said.

In the end, their boys found us. We were outside a chippy scoffing a typical match-day lunch of haddock and chips when this firm appeared. They came running down the street, giving it the big shout, but we ran them right back down the road. I was only a kid and I thought, great, we are really going to do them here. Eventually the cops appeared and kept us under watch until we reached the ground. They put us in a paddock. It was chucking down with rain and freezing cold. At the bottom of the terracing was an entrance tunnel and about 300 Middlesbrough boys appeared from it. They spent the whole game facing us, going wild, trying to get up the terraces. We kept running them back down, while the police struggled to contain both sides. Hardly anyone watched the game. The only thing I remember was a fan who ran on the pitch, rolled cartwheels and stripped off his clothes when they scored.

There was more scuffling after the match but we got back to the vans in one piece and got out of there. If we'd only filled up with petrol before the game, it would have been a good day. But we had to stop at a petrol station, and the attendant comes over and says, 'Have you been to the match, lads? What score was it.'

Someone said, 'One-nil, fuck off,' and hit him. A guy selling petrol. We jumped in the van and sped off but the police stopped us a bit further on. We were all questioned about the attack and two of the lads were arrested and fined.

I was fighting every week and getting away with it most of the time but when I did get caught, the charges were getting more serious. At Nottingham, after the fight with the rugby players (see Chapter Eight), we were walking to the ground and passed a filling station. We decided to rob it. We charged in and tried to open the till but the woman behind the counter threw her arms around it and wouldn't let go. One of the lads grabbed it and ripped it off the counter and the woman got a shiner. On the way out, I grabbed a little portable television and lobbed it through the window.

The police were alerted and were on the lookout for black guys. They stopped us when we got to the ground and brought the petrol station staff there in a car. They identified us and the Five-Oh nicked the whole coachload and escorted us to a police station in Derbyshire. They had us in the back yard and took us onto the coach one by one for questioning. We all denied it so they had an identity parade. Charlie Sow was standing in the queue and the woman identified him as having given her a black eye, although it was nothing to do with him. Charlie went nuts and shouted, 'It wasn't me, you fucking slag.'

A bizzie belted him across the face. We all put our heads down, trying not to laugh. Charlie was dragged out yelling, 'I haven't done anything.' I got picked out for putting the TV through the window and was charged with criminal damage. I went back a few weeks later and copped a fine.

My brother Chris was nicked at Shrewsbury, in the

early stages of the Guvnors. The police were watching us. We were approached by an undercover copper, some bloke who came from nowhere and said to us, 'Here you are lads, do you fancy a ruckie?'

We don't use that word in Manchester. I'd never heard it. He was clean-shaven and had on a nice new City hat.

I said, 'Come off it, you're a fucking copper, aren't you mate?'

'No I'm not.'

'You fucking are.'

'I'm not a copper, I'm not a copper.'

He was crumbling. You could see his bottle had gone. He even pulled his driving licence out to show us, as if that proved anything. We left him. Later, we saw him at the Guvnors court case. He was a copper. We should have done him in but he escaped by the skin of his teeth.

In the ground, some of the lads had an argument with some fellow City fans. Tempers frayed and a scuffle broke out. The police moved into the crowd and decided to nick Chris for kicking someone in the face, which was great, because I'd done it. I saw the police coming, got down on my hands and knees and crawled through the crowd out of the way. I stood up just in time to see our kid getting dragged out. He was going bananas.

They put him in a pre-fab hut at the back of the ground, handcuffed to a rail. City had taken about 4,000 there and we decided that at half-time, using the big crowd as a cover, we would get him out. We all got together and rushed this hut and started rocking it with him inside. The police came out and there was a bit of a battle. In the end we got baton-charged. Chris was charged and was kept on remand in a prison at Leicester for three weeks.

Generally when you were nicked, the dibble in the cells weren't too bad. They'd have a crack with you. Their attitude was, they're doing their job. Even today, if I did something wrong and got arrested, I'd accept it. They're human beings. If you hurt somebody, they'll hurt you back. I don't hate the police for that. It's a game and some you win, some you lose. I got another fine there.

The incident with the undercover police officer should have shown us that a net was closing in. But we were spinning out of control. The violence was too addictive. We were too into it to stop.

★　★　★

The other occupational hazard of the football hooligan is a good hiding – or worse. People have lost their lives through soccer violence. I have been punched and kicked more times than I can remember, but I only came badly unstuck twice, against Sheffield Wednesday and Aston Villa.

We played Wednesday at Hillsborough in the League Cup in August, 1979. City's fans were in an end with a wedge-shaped section of Wednesday fans in the bottom corner and a fence separating the two. After a bit of mutual abuse through the fence, we jumped over it. The Wednesday scarpered and we took the little end over.

After the match, the police were segregating the City fans to the train and to the coaches. Our mob broke away down a side street, walked along a road and there at the end was a very large gathering of Wednesday. We were massiviely outnumbered and we stopped. Donald said, 'Shall we have it here? This'll be a good rumble.'

So that was settled. There was a four-foot high banking around the corner so we ran up it and waited for them to come at us. It was like Custer's last stand. They were worked up about what had happened in the ground and they came at us like madmen. We had the advantage of being on the banking but they were fighting their way up, toe-to-toe. Some of the lads realised we were going to lose and got on their toes. But half of us wanted to see it through and Donald said, 'We're having it. Stay.'

Those that got of, got off, and those that stayed got done. I got done. A pack of them closed in on me and I started to get dragged off my feet. You always try to stay on your feet in a mass brawl because if you go down, you've had it. They were at me like a a pack of wild dogs.

I remember shouting out, 'I'm going down, I'm going down.' Then the world began to spin. What I didn't know, but everyone else could see, was that a big black Wednesday fan had pulled out a machete and started to fight his way through the crowd to get to me. Tony Dore, who was there, said it was the most frightening thing he has ever seen at a match. He was sure I was going to be butchered.

But as I have said, our Donald is scared of nothing. He saw what was about to happen and him and Tony ran into the Wednesday on their own to get me out. They fought off enough to get a gap in the crowd and legged it, dragging me with them. The guy with the blade never reached me, or I wouldn't be here now. We took revenge at the second was at our place. I believe a few of them were cut up.

Aston Villa have a lot of fans. They're good singers

but I wouldn't rate them as one of the hardest clubs. We played them in the late eighties, in the Guvnors era, in a Cup game (I always seemed to get nicked at Cup matches). It was midweek and we were at it all day in Birmingham city centre, smacking people, taxing a few shops, grabbing clothes or a bit of jewellery, like you do. One of our ploys was to arrive at the grounds late, so the other mob wouldn't think we were coming, and then attack them. On this occasion, it backfired. We got to the Villa Park at about ten to eight, well after kick-off. Fifteen of us were standing outside when a mob of 100 appeared. We ran down an alleyway and pulled a garden fence apart to arm ourselves. Then some daft bastard said, 'Split up.'

I said, 'Fuck off, stay together.'

But they all ran in different directions and it was every man for himself. Unfortunately, all the Villa came after me. I was running as fast as I could with this fence post but they caught up with me. I jumped into a garden and I tried to fend them off with the stick but I had no chance, there were too many of them. I didn't even manage to get a good hit on one. My feet went from under me and I was on the floor. I tried to roll in a ball, with fists and feet thudding into me. Then it all went black. I remember coming out of it, waking from a bad dream, and thinking, what the fuck's going on here? From somewhere a man's voice said, 'Are you all right mate?'

'Yeah, mate, sound. Help me up.'

'Well you've had fuck all yet, you Manc twat,' and with that the bloke ran up and whacked me again. I was sparkled. I must have been booted around while I was unconscious because when I finally woke up in a

Birmingham hospital my head was swollen like the Elephant Man's. I was covered in bruises, had stitches on my head and a couple of broken ribs. I finally got home two days later. The only consolation was that the rest of the fifteen had been kicked to fuck as well.

# 10
## *Cockneys*

THREE mobs in London stand above the rest: Millwall, West Ham and Chelsea. Like the Guvnors, their main gangs – the Bushwhackers, the Headhunters and the Inter-City Firm – were the targets of undercover police operations. They were luckier than us; the police fucked up. The court cases against most of them collapsed and their boys continued to terrorise the terraces. They are each awesome on their day. They also follow England en masse and have been responsible for a lot of the violence at internationals over the years. Any one of them is capable of turning over the others but overall I rate Chelsea top. They have got the numbers and are probably the best-organised firm in the country.

Although those three stand out, every team in London has a firm. We looked forward to playing in the capital: it was a day out and a chance for mischief. Sometimes we went down the night before and stayed over, but usually we'd spend Friday night in Manchester, go round the pubs, get kicked out of a club at 2am and then meet up at Piccadilly train station, where a coach would pick us up. We'd drive through the night down the motorway, people kipping, playing cards, drinking, and get to London at about 7am. By arriving early, we would miss the traffic, make a whole day of it and increase our chances of a rumble. We would stay until late in the evening, arrive home in the early hours and spend Sunday crashed out in bed. We were all young lads, no wives, no commitments. If you didn't go, you were a wanker.

We call all Londoners Cockneys, and we always found them game, especially on their own manor. The Cockneys are good snipers; they like to mingle in with you on the sly and kick it off. If they get too close you can get stabbed; that's why we kept the firm really solid when we went there. The fact that we all knew each other so well made us impossible to penetrate.

Usually we'd hit central London first for a drink. We always got sussed. The dress sense was beyond Manchester's. They would get stuff in the shops six months before us. Everywhere in Britain, the lads dress slightly differently, and in London we stood out because our clothes were different. In the casual era, and particularly toward the mid-eighties, the Mancs tended to dress down. Their boys were all fashion-conscious and we were, like, fuck it.

They'd spot you and you'd have battles all day. You'd get in a pub and they'd rush the pub. It was great. We didn't care what happened, as long as they knew we had been down there and caused problems. You could imagine them talking afterwards, 'Fuckin' hell, them Mancs did this, them Mancs did that.' That was what we wanted.

Despite West Ham's reputation, I have never rucked with them. Our Donald, however, had a couple of bad encounters with them:

*The only firm that did it at Maine Road in the early days was West Ham. They came up for a night game and got to the ground early. They went to the Platt Lane end and were milling round the turnstiles, acting like doormen.*

*Someone came and told me outside the ticket office. Most of our lot were already in the ground. I went round to Platt Lane, saw what was going on, got a little mob together and stormed the West Ham. They stood their ground. I managed to get over the turnstiles and fetch our lot inside. They all came running back down to the turnstiles and we saw them off. I remember a West Ham guy photographing me inside the ground, obviously for future reference. We used to have a cameraman as well, taking pictures of kick-offs and other firms.*

On another occasion, West Ham turned up at the Wimpy while Donald was working there. He had a row with them, went outside, the boss locked the doors behind him and the West Ham chucked him through the plate glass window.

In the eighties, West Ham's Inter-City Firm, so called because they used scheduled inter-city train services rather than football specials to travel to away matches, became one of the most notorious of all soccer mobs. They also had a younger offshoot, like our Young Guvnors, called the Under-Fives. Their name spread widely when they were the subject of a television documentary, although one part of it showed them coming off worst against United at Old Trafford; no disgrace, given the mass numbers you encounter there.

Their high-profile brought the Old Bill down on them and they were one of the first targets for the kind of investigation, this one called Operation Full Time, that was to be used against us. Twenty-six lads were arrested in the usual dawn raids by 250 police – that's nearly ten coppers for every fan. The papers described them as 'Britain's most feared gang of soccer hooligans.' In court, the cops claimed to have infiltrated the ICF. But doubts about the accuracy of the logs the officers had used to record their evidence meant the trial was stopped and the lads walked free in May, 1988.

The only time I went to Upton Park was the year before, on May 9, 1987. It was the game we needed to win to stay in the First Division and City took about 10,000. We had one of our best-ever firms out, nearly 400 on the train. We met early at Manchester Piccadilly; there was some building work there and the gaffer had left a white hardhat lying on the floor with 'Boss' written on the side, so I nicked it and wore it all the way down to London.

We got to Euston and made our way down into the tube station. About eighty of us crammed into a carriage on the first train to Upton Park and we set off. Some Chelsea fans got on at the next stop and one of them told us that if we went to a pub nearby we would find their firm. Someone pulled the emergency chord to stop the train. Unfortunately we were just out of the station and we couldn't get off. The police arrived and nicked me straight away, standing there in a hardhat with Boss on the side. I was taken out of the station and put on a coach waiting outside. One of coppers turned his tie round and showed me something pinned to the back of it. It was a West Ham badge.

'That's the facking team, mate,' he said.

The next thing, they were bringing the rest of them out as well. They filled two coaches. We were kept at a nearby police station until 4.30pm. We gave the cops loads of abuse but they weren't having it, they just said, 'There's no way you're going to the match and causing trouble, lads.'

They confiscated my hat, too. They knew who I was by then and as they let us go one of them said, 'Francis, get on the next facking train or you're getting nicked.'

Of course, I didn't. We pretended to go to the station and then headed into the West End to join the rest of the lads for a drink. We scattered around different pubs and had no bother with anyone. By now we knew that we had lost the game 2–0 and we were relegated. Some City fans who had been to the game turned up and said West Ham had been great, swapping scarves and applauding the City fans at the end. Which was all very nice, but we had to have a rumble. We were in London, so we had to kick someone's head in, didn't we?

When it happened, it was strange. We were drinking outside a pub when to two blokes across the road started singing, 'City's going down, City's going down.'

We were all asking each other, 'Who are these cunts?'

One of the lads threw a beer bottle at them and it shattered against a wall, showering them with glass. Instead of getting on their toes, they came over. One of them pulled out an ID card with a badge on it and said, 'Police.'

They were plain clothes London coppers, trying to get us at it, which happens sometimes. The guy with the warrant card tried to nick the bottle-thrower, there was a scuffle and the bizzie ended up on the floor. Then we did one before the back-up arrived.

I ducked into a pub with my mate Jimmy. We sat down next to two Cockney birds and started talking to them. Suddenly the door of the pub swung open and the heavy mob arrived with alsatian dogs, looking around.

I said to this bird, 'Look love, we're from Manchester

and we're going to get nicked. Can we pretend we're with you?'

They thought it was right giggle. We weren't spotted and the boys in blue left the pub.

We had arranged that if we got split up we would meet back at 10pm at Euston. When we got there, the rest of the lads told us that the cops had gone into another pub and found our Chris and a bunch of others. The two plain clothes guys were there but instead of nicking our lot, they started chatting. One said to Chris, 'That's the best kicking I've ever had. You're a good firm.'

Then he bought him a drink and they all went on their way!

While we were standing in the concourse at Euston, a load of supporters in red and white came walking through. They were Arsenal, on their way home from a game. We scattered them.

The cops were desperate to get us out of London and finally rounded us up on to a platform ready for the next train to Manchester. Once again, a train pulled in on another platform and we heard singing. It was a contingent of Man United fans, Kidderminster Reds, back from Old Trafford. We raced round and kicked them all over Euston Station. By now the Transport Police were totally cheesed off. They came in numbers, got us together, penned us up and put us on the next train out. We got back to Manchester about 3am. Apart from being relegated, it was a great day out.

Arsenal apparently have a tasty firm, the Gooners, although I have never seen any evidence of it. We went down there in the late seventies, arriving at 7am. We nicked a load of milk off doorsteps and hung around waiting for the pubs to open. We came across a load of

Queens Park Rangers, started talking to them and had a game of football with them in a park, one of the few times in my life when I have met rival fans without hitting someone. Then we went our way, they went theirs. We got to the ground at about 1.15pm. The City team coach was coming up the hill and all these Arsenal fans were coming down. The City players saw us and I swear a couple of them were mouthing, 'Go on lads, give it them!'

A few years later, we took one of their pubs. We went down on the train and piled into a boozer around the corner from Euston. The police arrived and one of them said, 'You lot had better fuck off, this is an Arsenal pub.'

'We ain't moving anywhere, mate, we're staying here.'

The bizzie thought this was quite funny and walked off saying, 'When the Arsenal come, they'll kick your arses all the way to the ground.'

Sure enough, before long a big firm of Gooners came down the street. We ran them down the road and the police, who had been lurking, waited until we had chased them and then baton-charged us. We ended up fighting the police and their fans, which is always a bit of a loser.

As I described in Chapter Two, we had a major battle with Spurs at home in which they put up a great show. I missed the cup finals against them. Donald took a big firm down to the first one at Wembley and leathered them. But at the replay they apparently murdered us; there were seventy-five arrests, mainly Spurs fans. I had problems with them once on Seven Sisters Road. I was with a mate called Chalky, a lad called Derek Lawlor and Izzy. We were in a pub having a drink with some City lads and a big Tottenham mob invaded it. We thought it best to leave and made our way out but they followed. A massive black guy was at the front of their mob.

Derek Lawlor had a sprained ankle at the time and said, 'I can't run.'

I said, 'Look behind you mate, you'll fucking run.'

He looked back and saw this black guy thundering towards us with a big mob behind him. Derek went flying past me with his sprained ankle, setting a new record for the 100–yard dash. We got chased off but none of us got caught. Sometimes you have to run. There's no point in standing there being brave when you're outnumbered ten to one and any football fan who says he has never run is a liar.

\* \* \*

When it comes to fear, there are few things to match being bushwhacked in a dark subway by several hundred Millwall boys. It makes you wonder why you ever became a football hooligan.

Our Donald rates Millwall as the best firm in London. He and some of the lads had a big ruck with them at the train station one year when we played Arsenal. I crossed swords with them in two of the most violent encounters the Guvnors ever had.

The first was on September 16, 1987. We were both in Division Two. There were some good firms there – Millwall, Middlesbrough, Leeds, Birmingham – and we all wanted to be top dog. So we planned a big ambush. It was a Wednesday night game and Millwall came on the train. They had a huge police escort to the ground and we couldn't get near them. After the game (we won 4–0, if anyone's interested), the cops locked them in the ground until 10pm. About 300 of us made our way to a small housing estate off Lloyd Street and gathered every milk bottle left on the doorsteps.

As we waited in the darkness, a lone police dog handler drove up in his van. We were all massed there, with everything you could think of to throw. There was no way he was going to stop us. Then we saw the Millwall escort coming down the road. We waited until they were about fifteen yards away and let fly. The sky filled with missiles. Millwall got on their toes and we ran them down Lloyd Street. The police baton-charged us but we ran right through them. Millwall are made of stern stuff, however. They stopped and came back at us. Lads were laying into each other right across the road. The police got together, sirens blaring and horses charging, and finally chased us off through the estate.

We knew there would be reprisals when we played the away fixture three months later. I expected a lot of lads to find excuses not to go but, as it turned out, we had a top mob. Their reputation was a magnet. We planned the trip in the pub and decided we would take the train, catch the tube to the Thames and then walk from there, right through their manor. To do that at Millwall would be the ultimate test.

Several hundred caught the train, while our mate Mikey Williams took a coachload from the Moss Side-Fallowfield area. Millwall knew we were coming. A few City fans in London knew us and the word went around that we were bringing a firm. We got off at Euston and caught the underground to London Bridge. I didn't know how long it would take us to walk from there and I didn't give a fuck. We were going to storm the Lions' Den.

We were coming up the steps from the tube station when we hear a low chant, dead slow.

'Mill-wall. Mill-wall.'

I said, 'Where the fuck's that coming from.'

We looked behind us and saw loads of them pouring through from another entrance to the station. They had been waiting for us. There was a shout of, 'Cam on, you northern barstards,' and they charged.

We ran up onto the street, stopped and turned and fought toe-to-toe for five minutes, a hell of a long time in a fight. It was dead even. We wouldn't give and neither would they. The police were nowhere; unbeknown to us, they had been tipped off as well and were secretly filming the whole incident. Finally they arrived in force, chased off the Millwall and pinned us in a corner.

They marched us along the Old Kent Road to the ground without any more trouble, although there were lots of horrible-looking thugs shadowing us, making throat-cutting gestures and trying to get in among us. The thing about Millwall, they don't do a lot of dancing up and down. They walk right up and whack you. It was nerve-wracking but an unbelievable buzz because we were there, on their patch, in one of the roughest parts of London, and it's up to them to come and do it. We tried to get away from the cops a few times and get into a pub but they wouldn't have it.

When we reached the ground, the Millwall made a last attempt to get at us. They went through the cops as if they weren't there and kicked it off at the turnstiles. We hit back at them and there was another skirmish before the horses came in. That was filmed as well – and would later be used as part of the court case against us.

The atmosphere inside the Den was utterly evil. At

least half of their fans did not watch the game at all. They spent the whole time baying at us, picking out individuals in the crowd and shouting out what they were going to do to us after. We did the same to them. To this day I don't know what the score was.

The police kept us in for half an hour but, even then, the car park was full of heads when came out, all faced in our direction. We were sure they were going to hit us but we had to put on a show. Everyone was geeing each other up, saying, 'Come on lads, stick together, let's have it.'

But really we were all thinking, who's going to walk at the front?

The cops, however, knew what was going on. They flanked us with a solid escort and took us all the way back to the tube. Some of the Young Guvnors had another ruck at London Bridge, nothing major, and we managed to get home relatively unscathed. Which was more than could be said for Mikey Williams's mob. Their coach was attacked and completely wrecked before the game. The driver was so scared that he fucked off and left them in London. But we had a good kick-off, no-one was nicked, no-one was hammered and we made our mark. That's the only time I've been to Millwall.

But of all the mobs I have encountered, perhaps the best was the one Chelsea brought to Maine Road on May 4, 1984. I had been to Chelsea several times, on coaches, and always had major problems. So I thought I knew what to expect when they came up for a Friday night match that would decide whether or not they were to be promoted from Division Two. We were ready for a ruck but we hadn't made any special arrangements. We had no idea what was about to hit us.

My first inkling came as I drove along Princess Parkway from my home in Wythenshawe. I intended to park near the ground and find the boys in one of our pubs. Away coaches used to park on my route, at Hough End, and as I neared the ground, the road was completely blocked by hundreds and hundreds of Chelsea. All the traffic was stopped. I thought, fuck me, I'm not going down that way on my own. I did a right turn down Withington Road, down to Oxford Road, parked at Rusholme and went into an Irish pub called the Clarence, where a lot of our boys used to have a pint before the game. Some lads I knew were outside and one of them said, 'Mickey, you can't go in there, it's full of Chelsea.'

'What are you talking about? It's our pub, I always go in here.'

I walked in. It was wall-to-wall Chelsea. I walked straight out again. We couldn't even meet in our own pubs.

They brought around 7,000 and they were nearly all boys. Around Maine Road it was murder; City were getting chased everywhere. I had never seen anything like it. We rounded up a mob of 100 and stuck together like glue. I broke my hand in a fight outside the ground and one of the Mayne Line, James Doherty, was nicked. But we couldn't take them on head-to-head; they had too many firms. There was more trouble in the city centre later, a woman got hit over the head with a pint pot in the Cyprus Tavern in Princess Street and a lad was slashed across the face in Platt Lane.

It can happen. If we were playing for the League

championship and we went down there, we'd take the ground over. When City played Newcastle in 1968, the last game of the season when we won the League, we filled virtually half of St James's Park. No-one is going to take a mob like that.

Our next experience with Chelsea was just as bad. In March, 1986, we reached the final of the Full Members' Cup, and played them at Wembley. It was a bullshit competition and City only took about 15,000 down there, which is crap for a Wembley final. The game was quite dramatic. Chelsea were stuffing us 5–1 but we scored three in the last ten minutes, finally going down 5–4. Off the pitch, City were obliterated. I think we were fighting the whole of London that day. Our mob went down about 200–strong, on coaches. We didn't get blitzed but all the goons got whacked. I remember the Chelsea fans butting the coaches, actually headbutting them and putting their fists through the windows. They were mad. Ninety-five people were arrested. Amazingly, a Scotland Yard spokesman told the papers, 'There was no serious crowd disorder. There was no damage to the stadium, no attacks on spectators in transit, no pitch incursion and no reports of injuries to spectators inside the ground.' It makes you wonder how twenty police were injured; two had to be kept in hospital overnight, one after being kicked in the mouth.

The Cockneys are very big on the England scene. I never watched England at all. Farrer and a lot of the white City lads did, and still do, but it's too right-wing for me. I felt that if I went, I might have got myself into a situation I didn't want to be in. When people are drinking, looking for a scapegoat, it doesn't matter how hard you are; if your own boys turn on you, you're finished. I didn't want to put my lads in a bad position where they had to choose between England and me. So I never got involved. But I'm proud to be English. I'm very pro-British but some people would not consider me English because I was black. Some football fans are very anti-black: Chelsea, Millwall, a lot of the southern clubs, Leeds; but a lot of them have more black players than we do. I watch England on telly but I always find it boring. I have never seen an exciting England team.

# 11

## *Guvnors*

IN January, 1986, a newspaper interview acquainted the law-abiding folk of Greater Manchester with a new menace: the Young Guvnors.

### SOCCER'S SECRET SQUADS OF SCUM

We call ourselves the Young Guvnors because although we're the youngest, we're the best. United have always been reckoned to be the trouble club but at City it's worse. United's hooligans are living on a worn-out reputation. They're rated in London but nowhere else. City's hooligans are rated everywhere. Wherever you go, other clubs' hooligans say, 'We heard what you did last week.'

On a good day there's fifty of us in the firm. We stick together and organise for away games. We meet in the morning, decide what train we will catch, where we will change and discuss who we are likely to meet on the way there and coming back.

Last season you could read about soccer violence every weekend. This season there's been hardly anything in the papers and it makes the public think it's under control. But it's not, it's still happening, everywhere. Every club has its hooligans, from the First Division down to non-League clubs. It's just a way of life. It's do or die.

The public's got the wrong idea. All the information they get is from the police. But there's two sides to every story. We want to stress that it isn't the innocent people we are after or who get hurt. It's the other teams' thugs. Heysel Stadium was ridiculous. We don't want anything to do with that. The Scousers mucked it up for everybody else. The police look at it this way, that since Brussels all of us – Manchester fans, Cockneys, whoever – are all murderers and that's turning everybody against us.

These quotes came from 'Kegs' – not his real name – one of a new, younger generation of City fans making their own mark on the hooligan culture of the eighties. The Young Guvnors evolved during the Mayne Line days. Guv'nor is a Cockney expression, meaning boss, and our seventeen and eighteen-year-olds wanted to boss their own little firm. They used to rip service stations apart; some of the older lads called them the Toffee Shop Stealers. They sometimes travelled with us but often did their own thing. They were sick of living in the limelight of others – and they were deadly. In the same article, two of them described some of the violence they had been involved in:

**Porstmouth, April 27, 1985**: The Pompey lads were standing round in groups of three or four. There were about 15 of us. We were walking along shouting: 'We are Mancs.'

We didn't know they had as many as they did. The Pompey lads came out of the station as we were going over the bridge and started giving it mouth. The inevitable happened – fighting started, blades were shown but not used. The Pompey lads were pushed back into the station and then the police came and broke it up. It was all over in a minute but our lads got the better of Portsmouth even though they were outnumbered.

**London Euston, November 2, 1985**: Our lads went into the pub and started smashing the place up. The Everton fans charged out – pint pots were flying everywhere. City started running at Everton and the Everton lads ran away. The cops came and lined us all up against a wall and searched us. No blades were found – a few had stashed their weapons beforehand.

Everton came back at us on the station looking for more. At first there were about 100 of our lads but then it was down to about thirty each. Our lads ran the Everton mob on to the platform and they started throwing hot drinks and British Rail signboards at us. The police came and made the Everton supporters get on the train home. But our lads stayed behind hoping some Arsenal fans would come to the station. They didn't – but three more Scousers turned up and there was more arguing.

**Leeds, generally**: They took liberties with eight of our lads once on a Bank Holiday trip to Blackpool. The Leeds hooligans attacked them on the prom. There was also a time when they battered a seven-year-old Man City fan and gave his dad a kicking when he covered him with his body to protect him. Manchester has hated Leeds for years since that. That was a case of innocent people being attacked and we get angry about that.

The Mayne Line, like the Cool Cats before it, finally folded. A lot of the older guys drifted away. Increased police attention and the new security measures being introduced after the Heysel Stadium disaster in May, 1985, including computerised membership schemes, alcohol bans and greater police surveillance, had an effect. At Maine Road, they installed cameras around the pitch, a cage to protect the players' entrance and replaced the neon-lit Manchester City FC sign above the main door because it kept getting smashed. People were also disillusioned with City on the pitch.

I was now twenty-seven, in my prime, known by everyone and able to round up the lads who were still interested. I don't remember exactly how the name Guvnors came about, but it may have been a piss-taking conversation with some of the Young Guvnors, along the lines of, 'You're not the fucking guvnors, we're the guvnors.' Anyway, the name stuck and, ironically, the firm really picked up when we went down to Division Two in 1987 and began to smash everyone in our path. Donald had moved away from the violence but Chris stayed with it all the way. If you look at the ages of those later nicked in the Guvnors case, there's only me and Chris and a couple of others over twenty-five. I was twenty-nine when I was sentenced. A lot of the main guys escaped the dragnet.

It was probably also important that I was one of the hardest in the mob. There was no-one in our mob I wouldn't have taken on. No-one has ever frightened me that way. I'd take on anybody and if I got beat, I'd leave it at that. But if someone took liberties, if I got knocked out and they smacked me to bits, stabbed me or whatever, then I wouldn't leave it, I'd carry it on. I'm from the old school; I don't use weapons, just my hands. I never thought to myself, I'm not going near him, he's too big. All the lads felt the same, invincible. Our song was: 'Ooh-ah, ooh-ah, Ooh to be a gov-er-nor.'

Despite my increasingly higher profile, they never tried to ban me at Maine Road. I was quite discreet inside the ground. We had moved from the Kippax now into the seats, about 300 lads. We had one section, A block in the North Stand, just for the Guvnors. Away fans would go in the Platt Lane End but their boys often went in the seats, although most of the violence now took place outside grounds where it was less likely to be detected.

All the arrangements, the meeting places, were sorted out by leading members of the firm. Everyone who needed to know would be told beforehand what was going down, by word of mouth. Sometimes you'd be let down by a poor turnout; then you'd get to your destination and loads more would join up with you there. Sometimes we made arrangements with people we were going to fight, talking through the fence at a match, passing phone numbers over, arranging where to meet after the game or telling the other side where to be when they came to our place. Even though you're sworn enemies, you can still talk to people. They were up for it as much as we were and everyone's goal was the same: kick arse.

The Guvnors were a hardened outfit. Many of us were veterans of hundreds of fights. We knew exactly what we were capable of. We didn't use weapons. Some might carry the odd blade but we didn't go out there saying, 'Right, we're all going to get tooled up tonight.' I think we were building up to be the main firm in Britain. We were doing the business and all the other firms, if they had anything about them, knew that on the day they played us they had to turn out or they were going to get run. And they were all turning out for us; it was kicking off every week. There was a challenge everywhere we went.

It was our firm looking for their firm. We weren't interested in anyone else. You can walk into a pub and you know it's not going to happen; go into the next one and you can sense it straight away. Dress code gives it away, people's body actions and charisma. You know they want it; they make it obvious. They're the ones that get a taste. If you see a bloke with two kids and a scarf on, you're not going to batter him. If you do, you're a cunt. But if you see six or seven lads and they want to have a go, yeah, have a go. I don't see anything wrong with that.

We'd use any mode of transport: trains, cars, vans, whatever. The coaches by then were well-known and the police kept stopping us on the motorway and giving us an escort. It was a waste of time going anywhere if you were going to be escorted to the ground, locked in, then escorted out again and home. You couldn't even get a beer, let alone a fight.

We had a great set of boys. Mad James was an Irish lad from Denmark Road. He always ran in first and he always got his nose bust. He used to wear a daft blue denim waistcoat. Dave Foulkes from Fallowfield was slightly built, had fair, mousey hair and a face like a squirrel. He worked at the Co-op in Ardwick. He was a good shouter, yelling, 'They're here, they're here,' until all the lads arrived.

Dave Israel from Fallowfield was still with me. His brother Paul was a hard bastard. I went to their house once before the match and Paul was standing behind the door. As I walked in, he jumped out, said, 'Here y'are, Mickey,' and spattered my nose with a punch. He thought it was funny. I'll get my one back one day! I played football with Dave on a Saturday and Sunday, went to the match with him on Saturday afternoon, we were pretty close. One particular match day, his dad was terminally ill, dying in bed at home. I went to the house and said, 'There's nothing you can do, Dave. We'll go to the match. It'll be all right.'

We left for the game and half an hour later, his dad died. We came back at tea-time and his mam went berserk at me. She hated me afterwards for that, blaming me for taking Dave to the match and missing his dad's last moments. It was pretty sad.

But Dave needed no encouragement. He was small, fiery and game. We played United one year and he went in their end, the Platt Lane, wearing his City shirt. One of his mates said, 'Take you're shirt off, Dave.'

'I'm City through and through and I'm not taking my shirt of in our own ground.'

I think he lasted five minutes before some United fans caned him. Dave was dead funny, good company to go away with. Like Charlie Sow, he was a jibber. He would go to the match without a penny in his pocket and jib all day. Jimmy Gittings was a pocket bull terrier. He would never run. Then there was Pat Berry. He had his own clique from Levenshulme but often came with us. He is well respected in his own right. When people talk about main City boys, his name always comes up.

Almost all of these lads were to be convicted in the Guvnors trial. Many others got away. Their names have never hit the headlines and that's the way they want to keep it. One lad who couldn't stay out of the papers was Donald Farrer. As I have already mentioned, he's from

Middleton and had a little firm of his own at one time. He got involved with our mob at the tail end. He was just a nutter. He would do mad things like go to Arsenal and go in their end on his own; the City fans could see all these fists going up and it's Farrer in the crowd getting smashed. He wore jeans with his arse hanging out, like a navvy. One year when we played Oldham, he was running down the street hitting man, woman and beast. He ran on a bus to punch a passenger but as he was about to jump off the doors closed and trapped him by the arm. Some blokes battered him. That was typical of Daft Donald. He wasn't part of the Guvnors case but he's been nicked dozens of times for football violence. He's been kicked to fuck that many times, he's got no sense left. He'll go into anyone, he's not bothered, doesn't think about it, just steams in.

Most of the teams in Division Two were rubbish. Oldham were no contest, although they have a firm, the Fine Young Casuals. Bradford City have the Ointment mob. We met a few boys there, a lot of Pakis and blacks, but we didn't have any problems. Stoke City, we always killed them. Shithouses. They thought they had a firm but they didn't, though apparently they're game now and murdered City when they played them last year. When we were going, we used to take the piss out of them.

Plymouth, I went all the way down there once, which is a hell of a long journey, but saw nobody, although apparently they have some real monsters, especially on their home ground. The Young Guvnors got up to some mischief when we played Plymouth at our place, as one of them, Vincent George, recorded in a diary that was later used at his trial:

When the match finished we all walked down to the Sherwood. On the way there four of us, me, Lee, Francey and Malcolm, battered about six Plymouth fans and then told them to fuck off. They ran away back to their van and drove past us.

By this time we were outside the Sherwood pub. All of the boys were getting firmed up to blitzkrieg the queers in town who were on the Clause 28 march. We did them top. We all splintered off into three small firms consisting of about ten in each. The firm I was in was the first to go in. We used weapons which we found lying about near the town hall and then we organised the ambush.

When we went in and started it off (we're the ones who always go in first to get the ambush started), by now we were tooled up with sticks, bottles, the metal insides of bins and cobblestones which were being pulled up by workmen. When my firm went in at the puffs we threw the bottles and stones and then ran in while the queers were still surprised at our actions. Then the queers started back at us. It was then the other two firms sprang the ambush. It went like clockwork.

Of the other teams we played that season, Blackburn Rovers showed us nothing, nor did Bournemouth, Ipswich Town or Bristol City, who are supposed to be handy. Some places, you can go there and, once they see there's a mob of you, they don't want to know, they crumble. I missed Leicester City away that season, having been arrested a couple of weeks before, but have been there several times and never encountered any trouble, although their Baby Squad are a very well-known and tasty firm. Hull City and Sheffield United have got a firm. So have Wolves. I went to Wolves that year and got on the pitch when City scored. The police filmed us.

The surprise package were Swindon Town. (You never know where you are going to get a surprise. Cambridge United's Main Firm smashed a load of Chelsea once.) We played them away on October 31 and only took a minibus; it was that far that no-one wanted to go, and they had no reputation. I think United were playing at home and quite a few wanted to stay in town and do them after their game, but we managed to round a tidy little mob up: Chris, Jimmy Gittings, Pat Berry, Skinner, twenty of us altogether. About 1,000 City made the journey. I don't remember the score. It was irrelevant to us most of the time. We would watch the match, get right behind the team, singing and everything, but at the end of the day you were just there for the buzz, to see what you could get away with before and after the match.

We had parked the minibus on a quiet side street. We got back there to find someone had punctured the tyres with a knife. We went to the chippy and were sitting there eating, wondering how the hell we were going to get back, when we heard this big roar. A hundred Swindon fans came sprinting round the corner. They took us completely by surprise and we retreated in some disarray. They chased us up the road and smashed all the windows in the minibus – so now we've no tyres and no windows. That pissed us off. We turned and ran back at them in this narrow terraced street and had a tit-for-tat for a good ten minutes before the police turned up. All the neighbours were at the windows, watching the free show. The Swindon chased us down one end of the street, we chased them back, everyone was getting smacked. They were mainly young lads but they were game and we took a lot of punishment. My arse was going a bit but in the end the twenty of us did them. Finally the police got between us and chased the Swindon off. They sent for another minibus. It came from somewhere and they towed the other one away. We got an escort to the motorway at 10pm.

We were far more familiar with another team we played that year: Huddersfield Town. We played them twice in the League and three times in the FA Cup that season. After beating them 10–1 at Maine Road, we weren't expecting much of a contest at the Cup match in January and decided not to go. But City were taking a mob so, on the day, I said to our kid, 'Shall we go or what?'

Chris was up for it. He had been arrested at the 10–1 game for steaming into the Huddersfield escort and had missed the biggest win in City's history; the Bill kept going down to his cell to tell him the score and he wouldn't believe them. So the pair of us and Jimmy Gittings went across the Pennines in my car. We got to a little cafe for something to eat and sat facing the window. In the street we could see these two black guys with a firm of about fifty lads. They were smacking every City fan that went past, scarfers, ordinary fans, dads and mams. We made a mental note of their faces.

We went for a wander but missed City's main firm and fell in with a load of nobs, the idiots. We couldn't bear to walk to the match with a bunch of civilians so we left them and walked up this road, just the three of us. It was raining and I had a brolly. We got across by a pub and there were the fifty Huddersfield outside, chanting, 'Hudders, Hudders,' or something like that. The two black lads were with them.

We had no colours on but they sussed us straight away. We stood on the opposite side of the road, with them staring at us and us staring at them. Then our kid said, 'Shall we have a do with them?'

'Are you fucking mad, Chris? There's only you, me and Jimmy.'

'Come on, let's have it with them.'

So I thought, fuck it, let's have it. We walked across the road and ran into them. For some reason they all went for Chris and he went down. I came through with the brolly to save him. The police were on to it straight away and separated us. The officer in charge shouted, 'Right, all you City fans over there, Huddersfield over there.'

Then they realised there was just three of us. You could see them looking at each other, saying, 'No way, there's got to be more of them than that.'

The police took the three of us over to the kerb and were deciding what to do with us when one of the Huddersfield ran out of the crowd and whacked Chris on his ear. It must have stung like mad because it was a cold day. He was going off his head.

The police put us on a bus to the ground with a load of other City fans. Inside, we met up with the boys. Everyone was talking about Huddersfield taking the piss and whacking all the goons in. So after the match we went on the warpath. We had parked our car near the train station so we would be walking back all together – and who did we walk into but the Huddersfield lads. They came round a corner and bumped into us, the two black kids walking at the front. To cut a gruesome story short, their firm got destroyed. We took over the town centre and stayed all evening drinking, about eighty of us. No-one would come near us.

The game was a 2–2 draw. We replayed the next Tuesday at Maine Road, drew again, and had to go back to their place the following Monday. This time they had their whole firm out. They really wanted to know but we did them in again. They're just pie-eaters.

Middlesbrough were also in the division. They still have a good firm now. One of my mates who supports Man United went up there last year. United had eighty boys surrounded by 500 Middlesbrough. They refused to back off and had it toe-to-toe with them at the train station. At the end the police came between them and the Middlesbrough clapped United's mob for sticking it.

I went to West Brom on November 28, 1987. The Guvnors were there for a piss up really because, as far as I am concerned, West Brom are fuck all. We got drunk and went round their end. At the turnstiles, a copper said, 'Where are you from, lads?'

Someone said, 'Birmingham,' trying to put on their dopey accent.

'Which part of Birmingham?'

The guy repeated some daft place name he'd seen on the way down. Whatever it was, it worked, because the copper let twenty of us in before he tumbled and stopped the rest. I made my way to the toilets, thinking about fifty of us have got in. There was a guy in there who looked a bit of a boy, so one of the lads smacked him and said, 'Go on, you fucking Brummie, get your boys.'

He ran out and we moved onto the terraces. Within thirty seconds, everyone knew we were there. We worked our way towards the bottom of the terrace and the crowd started swaying and grumbling. The City fans in the away end noticed us and started singing, 'City aggro, City aggro.'

All their boys finally popped up. You could tell us apart: we were all baseball caps and bomber jackets, they were scruffy bastards. Anyway, they rushed us. We fought them off and moved down into the bottom corner to find room to manoeuvre. They kept coming. I went for the front two, got caught against a barrier and took a couple of smacks in the mouth. We stood there offering them out but although the whole crowd was moving in on us, none of them would really go for it. Then the police came in, opened a gate in the fence and took us out of the ground. We were chuffed with ourselves but thought we were set for a night in the cells. Yet they didn't nick us. We couldn't understand why. It was to be several months later that we learned the reason. Once again, they were secretly filming the whole thing, to build a conspiracy case against the Guvnors. After the match, we decided to go round to their end. We were later charged with riot for that. We got towards their end and they saw us and legged it. They didn't want to know. The police got us together and within half an hour we were on our way home on the coach.

For me, we were now the main firm; we were just arrested too early to prove it. We had done all the Second Division and were starting on Division One, where the real firms are, when we got banned. We never had a chance to test the waters and we wanted it so much we were hungry for it. We had a massive firm and we were brewing up for a massive season.

# 12
## Operation Omega

I realised the Old Bill were on to us about six months
before we were arrested. There was a lot of pretty
obvious police observation: cops pointing cameras at us,
mysterious geezers standing in the crowd with earpieces
in, or sitting in the seats, pretending they were thugs,
wearing brand new City shirts. The real boys only wore
little badges. Then there was the guy no-one knew who
approached us and said, 'Do you want to go for a
ruckie?' What's a ruckie?

The undercover operations began in the mid-eighties.
After Heysel and the European ban on English clubs,
Maggie Thatcher clearly took a decision to do something
about the football hooligans who were tarnishing the
country's good name and all that bollocks. The word
must have been passed on forcefully to the various chief
constables around the country. I think Maggie had had
enough. There was violence all the time, it was going on
and on. We were running riot.

The first to go were the big London clubs. In May,
1987, several alleged leaders of the Chelsea Headhunters
were jailed (they later got off on appeal). Cases were
also pending against more Chelsea, Millwall, West Ham,
the so-called Para Army at Leeds and Oxford United's
South Midland Hit Squad. Everyone was hearing whis-
pers that something was going down in Manchester. Still
we carried on, partly because we were allowed to. I think
the police purposely left us to it to build their case. They

were watching all the time. Some of it we were aware of and some we weren't but we'd had a free-for-all for ages and we just wanted it to go on.

Manchester police would travel away with the City fans because they knew the troublemakers. They'd film supporters from the train station to the ground, quite openly, standing right in front of you. Obviously they were getting a dossier together to build a case. Most of the video evidence used against us at the trial didn't show fighting but simply who associated with who. There's not much violence on the videos. However, a lot of the things that the police came up with in their statements about fights were very accurate. Some of the things we got up to, they were obviously with us.

They didn't get into the crew as such; they latched onto fringe members of the firm. There was one lad called Mark Chapman who turned the case. Chapman was from Didsbury. He wasn't really one of the main lads but used to team up with us. Our Chris knocked him out once. We were playing Charlton away; there was a bit of a conversation on the coach and he made some remarks about Chris, something about a situation where it had kicked off and Chapman said, 'Chris's arse went.' Chris it took pretty badly because he is not is a runner. They met up at a service station, Chapman's walked over with a few lads like he was going to do the business and Chris has knocked him out clean.

Chapman more or less threw his hand in and blew everybody up. He's never been seen since, not since 1989, and I don't know where he is. He got a suspended sentence in the end although he had been well involved in the trouble. Apparently, he met these three lads who said they were City fans from Blackpool. They were actually undercover CID. I had nothing to do with them. Most of the guys I knocked around with were life-time mates. But Chapman got on with them very well. The police bugged a car and whenever Chapman got in it and was talking, he was building himself up, saying, 'We've done this and I've done that.' He put himself in the shit.

The coppers were asking things like, 'Who's this lad here, what's this Mickey Francis like?'

'Ooh, he's a fucking nutter, him,' Chapman would say.

'Has he got a firm? And who's this lad, has he got a firm?'

They were sussing everyone out, pretending that they were would-be hooligans who wanted to know the main faces. Chapman, unknowingly, was giving them the information. The police would leave after matches, saying they were going back to Blackpool, and would drive straight to a safe house and write up their notes.

I'm 100 per cent sure that they never got into the main firm. They were on the fringes. A lot of times, they let things happen, to make their case. For example, when we went to West Brom and kicked off in their end, we didn't get arrested; Millwall, same again. They weren't bothering to nick us for single offences, they were making a conspiracy case, building it up so we would be bang to rights. In January, 1988, we had serious ructions at Everton and against Aston Villa at home. Again, no-one nicked. In the first week of February, police swooped on homes in north London and the Home Counties and lifted sixteen alleged members of Arsenal's Gooners gang. The cops said they were moving to prevent planned trouble at the Arsenal and Manchester United

FA Cup tie on February 20. The fans were charged with violent disorder. The net was getting tighter.

\* \* \*

Early Thursday morning, February 11. It is still dark. I'm asleep in bed at my house in Prestwich. There is a knock at the front door, then some loud thumps as it is smashed in before anyone can answer. I jump out of bed, peer through the window and see police outside. I run to the back and look into the garden and they are there as well. With me being the so-called Guvnor, they've sent a right firm down there, thinking I'm going to kick off. But I'm not going to cause a scene with a bunch of TAG boys, all hyped up and wanting to kick arse. The Five-Oh rush up the stairs. Funnily, as they come in the phone goes. It's one of the lads, ringing to warn me he's getting raided. A copper answers and says, 'It's okay, he knows we're here!'

They come in the bedroom and cuff me. I want to go for a shit so they let me in the bathroom with the door open. I'm sitting there, dropping my guts in public, thinking, so fucking what? I'm allowed to shit in my own house. They let me have a quick shave and get dressed. All the while, they were saying, 'Well, you've fucked it now mate, we've got you on camera, you're going away for a long time.' Yeah, yeah, yeah.

They look under the stairs and find a carpet knife which I use in the house. One of them pulls it out, dead excited, and shouts, 'Exhibit one, we've got a Stanley knife!'

'Have you used that at football matches?'

'No.'

As if I'm going to say, 'Yeah.' They put it in a plastic

bag and mark it 'Exhibit One.' One of them finds a wooden cosh under the bed, brings it out and says, 'Ooh, what's this?'

'It's a fucking cosh, in case I get broken into, I can do someone in with it, you know. Everyone has something in the house.'

Well, haven't you?

It's not an offensive weapon until it's outside your house. I know the score. They take it and bag it. Next they get to my toolbox. They bring a claw hammer out, put it in a bag, a ball hammer, various other tools, saying, 'You use all these at football matches.'

I can now see what is going on. They're looking for anything to pin on me.

'That's my fucking toolbox, I'm in the building game, I'm a scaffolder. I do buildings all day long.'

'No, we know you've used these at football matches.'

The cops lead me out of the house and drive me to Longsight police station. They sit me down and ask me endless questions. I give them back, 'No comment.'

'Did you go to this match on this day?'

'No.'

'Well, you did, because you were seen and we've got photographs.'

'No comment.'

They interview me about six times during the day, on and off. They'll go away, then come back and start laying it on.

'Tut, tut, you've fucked it now mate, they've all stuck you in it. We know you're the main man.'

'I know I'm not the main man.'

I'm processed, refused bail and remanded to Strangeways.

The papers had a field day. This was the front-page report in the *Manchester Evening News*:

## GANG-BUST POLICE HOLD CITY FANS

Police investigating soccer violence at Manchester City raided more than 100 homes in Greater Manchester and Lancashire today after undercover work by detectives who infiltrated notorious soccer gangs called the Guvnors and the Young Guvnors.

Dangerous weapons were seized and twenty people were arrested in the dawn swoop which followed a secret six-month operation codenamed Omega. A task force of 100 officers was investigating alleged offences of wounding, theft and conspiracy to cause violent disorder.

A frightening array of weapons including flick knives, hammers, coshes and body armour has been recovered. Police also seized gang 'calling cards' which thugs leave with battered victims saying: 'You have just been done by . . .'

Arrests were made in Manchester, Oldham, Bury and Denton and other towns in the North West. One of those detained is a man wanted in connection with an incident at the City–Crystal Palace game at Maine Road last December 5 when a match official was seriously injured. He is thought to have been hit by a coin.

Today's swoops follow raids last week on twenty-six homes in North London and the Home Counties. Sixteen supporters have appeared in court on violent behaviour charges.

The Guvnors – many with well-paid jobs – are

understood to have planned trouble at away matches while the Young Guvnors carried it out.

Chief Supt Eric Tushingham, a veteran of crowd control at Maine Road, said: 'We have had few problems at City in recent seasons, but a small minority have seemed bent on spoiling the atmosphere. This operation was all about weeding them out.'

Operation Omega was led by Det Chief Supt Frank Halligan, GMP's head of support services. It is understood inquiries were made at almost every Second Division ground.

City chairman Peter Swales praised the operations and spoke of his disgust for thugs. 'They are not supporters,' he said. 'Obviously I am very disappointed that they apparently latched on to City.'

The guy arrested at the airport was heading to Israel for the England game the next week. The *Daily Mail* reported that 'detectives are investigating worrying links between the thugs and the National Front,' which was news to me. They also claimed that some of the gang were former Man United thugs who changed their allegiance to City because United's games were too well policed, which was bollocks as well. Another one of the papers referred to the Guvnors as 'respectable older men in well-paid jobs' and said cards had been left on battered bodies with the inscription, 'You have just met the Young Guvnors.'

By the end of the day, twenty-one people had been charged. They included our Chris, Pat Berry, Jimmy Gittings, Dave Foulkes and Rodney Rhoden from the Young Guvnors. Most were charged with conspiracy to commit riot or violent disorder at football matches. Me,

Chris and Mark Dorrian were charged with causing a riot at the match against West Brom the previous November. Several of the others faced a similar charge for an attack just eighteen days earlier on Aston Villa fans in Manchester. One lad was charged with impersonating a police officer with intent to deceive in Plymouth. Stephen Montague, from Blackpool, who was one of those the undercover coppers had befriended, was charged with a serious wounding offence for hitting referee John Deakins with a coin at the home game against Crystal Palace. As for 'respectable men in well-paid jobs,' most of the lads were either unemployed or had routine jobs like catering assistant, warehouseman, labourer, cellarman and driver. Two of the lads were only fifteen and sixteen and were legally classed as juveniles.

We were all to be taken to the City Magistrates Court in Manchester the next morning. Some were kept overnight in Strangeways and some in a detention centre. Then they loaded us into a van and we were on our way to court singing songs, 'Here we go, here we go, here we go.' It was the first time we had been together since being nicked and we began to realise the scale of the operation. Loads of cops and journalists were at court. We were put in the dock and they began reading the charges and outlining the investigation.

'Mr Francis, he's the main Guvnor, he's twenty-seven years old, a responsible person, he shouldn't be doing this. We raided his house in the morning and found these weapons.'

I looked at them and thought, this is a fucking set-up. They produced a crowbar, a ball hammer, a claw hammer and a Stanley knife.

'We have evidence that this man has used these things

at football matches. He is a danger to society. He has to be remanded in custody.'

My brief couldn't say much because it was just the start of the case and he didn't know what the fuck was going on. None of us had an idea of how strong the case against us was. So I was remanded to Strangeways, with Chris and five or six others. Almost everyone was in custody for the first weekend. The following Friday, eleven of us were refused bail again while the rest were let out on condition that they didn't go within half a mile of a League ground.

Things soon took a turn for the worse. On Saturday, February 20, there was a bloody confrontation at a train station in Manchester that became known as the Battle of Piccadilly. City weren't playing that day, so a firm of Guvnors and Young Guvnors gathered in town to attack United fans when they came back from a game in London against Arsenal. A copper who tried to stop them was badly hurt, as *The Sun* reported:

## COP FIGHTS OFF 60 SOCCER YOBS

Hero policeman John Duffy took on a mob of SIXTY soccer thugs single-handed to protect fellow officers.

As John, thirty-six, held off the horde, he was smashed on the head with a bottle [actually it was a hammer – M.F.], then knocked to the ground and given a merciless kicking.

Father-of-two John, a British Transport policeman, suffered a fractured skull. He later needed an emergency operation to remove a bone that was pressing on his brain.

Last night he was 'stable' in hospital. One of his

senior officers said: 'It was a horrifying experience and John was extremely brave.'

PC Duffy and his two colleagues, PCs Steve Martin and Darren Yates, were on a 'soccer special' train escorting Manchester United fans home after their FA Cup defeat by Arsenal on Saturday.

As the fans left Manchester's Piccadilly station some were ambushed by hooligans thought to be rival Manchester City fans.

PC Martin, thirty-two, was hit in the eye by one of the mob. As he and PC Yates, twenty-five, tried to arrest the attacker, the mob turned on them.

PC Yates was hit with a bottle and pushed over. Brave PC Duffy, a six-foot-tall ex-Army corporal, shielded his colleagues from the flailing fists and boots and saved them from further injury.

At least they couldn't pin it on me because I was safely tucked up in HM Prison Strangeways. But incidents like these were sure to stick in the public's and the judiciary's minds and count against us. The cops were now seriously out to get the remaining Young Guvnors and studied some of the secret film taken in our investigation to see if they could identify the Piccadilly mob. On February 24, they arrested another person in connection with Omega and in March they nicked seventeen lads, average age nineteen, for the Piccadilly incident, including Pete Frith, my mate who got his face slashed by the Scousers. The charges against eight of them were eventually dropped but the rest went for crown court trial.

I was in Strangeways for several weeks. Although I knew a lot of people in Strangeways and didn't find it hard going, it wasn't a pleasant experience. Fortunately,

I was in a cell with my brother. They put brothers together a lot and I think it's a good thing. You are weak in jail, no matter how strong you think you are. People try to put up this picture that jail is nothing but when that door shuts at night-time, you're on your own, your mind's working overtime, paranoia setting in. It does get to you. I passed the time reading and using the gym.

Finally my barrister made an application for bail before a judge in chambers. I waited all day for the result. It got to 6pm and there was a knock on my cell door.

'Francis, get your kit, you're going home.'

I jumped around like a madman.

'Pack your kit and have it in front of you in five minutes.'

That five minutes seemed like five hours. The screw came back and escorted me outside and through the yard. I could hear our Chris shouting. I shouted back, 'Chris, I've got bail.'

The others hadn't had their hearings yet but in the end they all got bail. The case took another year to reach court. All of that time, I was being told I was going to get seven years, which is a lot of stress. Even if you are wrong in what you have done, and deserve to be in there, there is still a lot of worry and pressure.

Nineteen eighty-eight was the year the silly inflatable bananas appeared at Maine Road. By this time, the new Ecstasy culture was also sweeping the clubs and a lot of lads were getting into peace and love and all that crap. Not, however, our firm. In May, the Young Guvnors struck again, this time at Old Trafford when City played United in a testimonial for the Reds defender Arthur Albiston. The Bill were waiting for it and filmed a fight in Chester Road.

On June 28, we were all indicted to appear before Manchester Crown Court. By this time, there were twenty-six of us. I didn't even know half of the younger lads. All but one were on bail and we were trying to keep a very low profile but, even then, the Guvnors couldn't stay out of the news. That balloon Donald Farrer was over in Germany for the European Championships and mouthed off to reporters in a bar. The next day he was pictured on the front page of the *Daily Star*, surrounded by glasses of lager and smoking a fat cigar, under the headline, 'I'M GOING TO KILL A KRAUT!' According to the story, he was going to 'do' the Russian goalie and also murder a German. He was wearing a tee-shirt emblazoned with a picture of Winston Chruchill and the words 'Two World Wars and a World Cup.' He also showed the reporter a knife hidden down his sock and told them he was from a gang called the Guvnors. Not surprisingly, he was later picked up by the German police and kicked out of the country.

In September, there was yet another major off at our home game against United. In November, Stephen Montague, the lad charged with throwing a 2p coin – cheapskate – at a ref, got a fifty-six day suspended sentence. He was cleared of wounding but admitted assault. The ref needed two stitches in his head. His case was somewhat weakened by the fact that he had asked an undercover copper for an alibi when he realised he might have been caught on video. In January 1989, twenty-six Blues were arrested when fighting broke out on the terraces during a Cup game at Brentford.

While on bail, I obeyed the order not to go to matches. I was too well known to break it. I also stopped running with the lads. I knew it was a high-profile case and I would probably go to jail. It wasn't worth the risk, so I stayed away. But the more that football violence was in the news, the worse it was for us. I was looking down the barrel at a long stretch.

# 13
## *Trial*

'MICHAEL, it's not looking too good. If we go through with the trail, you are facing six to eight years. If you throw your hand in now, okay, the judge will take it that you are the main man. That's bad for you. But he knows that you can swing it for the others to plead guilty if you do. That will count in your favour. If you jack it in, you are looking at a lower sentence and so are the others, as they all have to get less than you. At the end of the day, I think I can get you three years if you plead guilty.'

This inspiring little speech came from my barrister. He looked out of the window of the interview room in the new Liverpool Crown Court building. In the distance I could see a ferry crossing the Mersey towards Birkenhead, and the Irish Sea stretching out to the horizon.

He turned back to me. 'Take a good look, Mike. The way things are, you won't be seeing that again for seven years.'

Thanks very much, you bastard.

We were all pleading not guilty, but my chances of getting off were receding. The police had requested permission to give evidence while hidden behind screens. They didn't want to identify themselves, they said, because they were involved in dangerous undercover work. Naturally, I thought it was pretty sad that the justice system could let them get away with that sort of thing. They're police officers and they're getting paid to do a job. Testifying behind screens, hidden from the public gallery, gives the jury the impression that the defendants are a bunch of desperadoes.

One of those coppers was asked the question, 'How would you describe Mr Francis?'

His exact words were, 'He's a bully.'

Not, he's this tall, brown skin, stocky build, or whatever. Just, 'He's a bully.' It's not exactly evidence, is it? They were allowed to get away with things like that and, of course, they were granted their protective screens.

There was the odd funny moment. When we were asked to plead, the court clerk went through each of us in turn.

'Michael Francis, how do you plead?'

'Not guilty.'

Next.

'No guilty.'

And so on. It came to Martin Townsend. Martin has a speech impediment and we knew he wouldn't be able to get the words out.

'MartinTownsend, how do you plead?'

Before he could open his mouth and stutter, we all shouted in unison, 'NOT GUILTY!'

The whole court jumped about a foot in the air. We cracked up.

The trial began in February 1989 and was to drag on for months, a complicated mess of different defendants with different pleas. First up were two of our lads and one United fan, who admitted taking part in a fight outside Old Trafford. This was the brawl on Chester Road before Arthur Albiston's testimonial, three months after the original Guvnors arrests. Another City lad,

Vincent George, a seventeen-year-old who kept a written diary of his fights entitled 'War Games,' went not guilty. During his trial, the jury watched a three-minute black-and-white video of the fight, which took place in the middle of the road as cars swerved out of the way:

A jury retired to consider a soccer hooligan case today – all twelve members also witnesses to the alleged crime.

For the six men and six women at Manchester Crown Court had seen several times over a video recording of an incident in Chester Road, Old Trafford – shot by police spy cameras – when rival supporters clashed. The confrontation left one young fan unconscious on the ground, after being kicked and stamped on.

The surveillance equipment picked up a group of City fans walking towards Old Trafford forty-five minutes after the match started. 'The prosecution say their purpose was to fight – it wasn't to watch the match otherwise they wouldn't have been there at that time of the day,' said Mr Wright.

The group was seen by a 'scouting party' of United fans and various youths were spotted picking up missiles and arming themselves with sticks, he told the jury. Then the two groups clashed. Missiles were thrown, there was a large scale disturbance and one youth was left unconscious. Eventually the City fans turned and began walking away chanting and shouting.

Mr Wright said George had not kicked or fought with anyone but he was a member of a gang 'bent on trouble.'

For Mr George, Mr John Bonney said his client accepted he was guilty on the lesser charge of fear or provocation of violence, which carried a much lesser maximum sentence. Mr Bonney invited the jury to consider what they had seen on the three-minute clip of video, which showed his client had not thrown anything, hit, kicked or stamped on anyone.

'Had he intended serious violence, he had ample opportunity to carry it out, as others did. But he didn't.'

Mr Wright said that in an interview with the police Mr George had refused to identify any members of the City supporters gang, 'the Young Guvnors,' said to be involved.

'If I did that I would probably get my head kicked in,' George had told the police.

George's defence failed and he got three months for violent disorder. Rodney Rhoden, who was sixteen at the time and who jumped on a United fan's head as he lay on the floor, pleaded guilty and was sent to a young offenders institution for six months. The video was later seen by millions when it was shown on the national TV news.

Things went from bad to worse. On April 15, ninety-four Liverpool fans died in a crush in the Leppings Lane enclosure at Hillsborough in Sheffield. The whole world was shocked and there we were, about to go on trial a week later for football violence. We were fucked. By now, I was also much better acquainted with the evidence against me. It was pretty damning. At West Brom, I was caught clearly on camera having a punch-up with a couple of guys in their end. You could see me against a barrier getting caught briefly and them whacking me. Then we're on the pitch, all going, 'City, City,' like a little mad army, about twenty of us, and the police take us into our own end.

Another example was a home night match against Middlesbrough. I had been getting some chips and someone smacked me on the jaw. These Middlesbrough fans had parked their van up and jumped out and we had a little kick-off. I kung-fu'd one of them in the face on the forecourt outside the ticket office. As the rest of them rushed me, I slipped and got a bit of a kicking. I read the coppers' version of this in their statements and it was absolutely spot on; they must have been right there. Although none of them had actually got to know me personally, they had clearly come pretty close.

I was concerned, though, that if I went guilty, the next person down would then be named as the main man. That meant our Chris would have been labelled the Guvnor or, if he pleaded guilty, it could have been Dave Foulkes, or Martin Townsend, or Adrian Gunning. Then they would have been hit the hardest. If you looked at the charges, in that particular season I only went to twelve games. I only picked the games I wanted to go to. But they were more or less making out that every time it kicked off, it was down to me. The Guvnors were 100–150 strong but they picked a few of us, who they thought were the main players, and a few younger lads. I didn't even go to every game but they depicted me as being a figurehead: older than everyone else, a long criminal record, a reputation, a bit of a hothead. They said, 'It's got to be down to him, so make him the leader.'

That was when I got the little lecture off my barrister, who was actually very good, spelling out exactly what I was facing. Seven or eight years sounded an awful long time to risk for a not guilty plea, especially as I was guilty as hell. I knew there would be little point in carrying on once the jury had seen me brawling on video. My main concern became, not whether or not I was going to be convicted, but what sentence I faced. I knew I was looking at a long term because football violence was such an issue in the media and in Parliament. Everyone was saying, 'Mickey, it's looking like you're the main man, you're getting slammed with it.'

Fuck it. I changed my plea to guilty and so did most of the others.

On April 24, twenty-six of us appeared before Liverpool Crown Court. Twenty-one pleaded guilty but five went not guilty on the conspiracy to riot and cause violent disorder: Adrian Gunning, aged eighteen, Dave Foulkes, twenty-five, Andrew Bennion, twenty-one, David Goodall, twenty-three, and Ian Valentine, twenty-six.

The prosecutor, David Sumner, opened the case. He said the Guvnors and Young Guvnors had about thirty key members. He went on, 'There existed a hard core of people associated with this club whose sole purpose was violence for violence's sake – recreational violence. If they were meeting another particularly notorious group like Leeds it would attract them to a near organisational frenzy. They would put other members under maximum pressure to attend the games and swell their numbers.'

Some of the gang never even went to the match at home games, he said.

'They adjourned to a public house and assembled again shortly after the whistle. Their purpose was to attack, intimidate and terrorise.'

He said an undercover police operation against us was launched in August, 1987, using officers for a specially trained unit codenamed Omega.

Then one of the covert officers, referred to by the pseudonym Mr Henry in court, gave evidence from behind the screen. He claimed he was running with us for seven months, going to away matches and sometimes acting as a van driver after being accepted. He said that as part of Operation Omega, he and three other detectives took on new identities, with disguises and fictional names and addresses. After each match they would return to a 'safe house' to write their reports. They also used codenames for their targets: Gunning was Alpha, Foulkes was Nobby, Valentine was Heron and Goodall was Duck.

As well as trotting out the line about the Young Guvnors acting as spotters at railway stations and reporting back to us, he also said some of them, described as 'baby-faced' and aged between fourteen and twenty, would position themselves next to police officers to listen in to radio messages, allowing them to find out the movements of opposing fans and so work out the best place for an attack. He said they would also watch any spectator who reacted to an opposition goal, marking him out for treatment.

The newspapers were taking a big interest. This was the *Daily Mirror*:

## VIOLENT WORLD OF THE SOCCER GUVNORS

A gang of soccer thugs plotted vicious fights with

rival supporters like a company ran its business, a court heard yesterday.

The gang, attached to Second Division Manchester City, had two branches – the Guvnors and the Young Guvnors, Liverpool Crown Court was told.

It was alleged that they:

- Marshalled like an army, using scouts to watch the movements of rival fans;
- Remained anonymous by hiding their faces from monitor cameras at grounds;
- Grouped ready for attacks in pubs without seeing a second of any soccer match.

The gang was finally smashed by undercover detectives who penetrated the secret world.

And so on. Tempers occasionally boiled over. The *Manchester Evening News* was snatching pictures of everyone going in or out of the court and Adrian Gunning, who was a top lad in the Young Guvnors, lost his rag. He told the photographer to hand over his film, tried to smash his camera and apparently threatened to slit his throat. The photographer reported it to the judge, although he didn't name Adrian. The judge said he was 'outraged' and said anyone else who threatened the Press, who were there to report the case for the public, would be remanded until it was over. He gave a little speech, saying, 'In any democracy the Press are the lamps which show justice is living. They are welcome in this court. If anyone approaches the Press they will have the full rigours of the law brought down by me. If I have a hint of it happening again, substantive periods of imprisonment will be imposed.'

So Adrian was told to keep his fucking mouth shut because no-one wanted to go back inside.

According to a report of the trial in *The Sun*, the Young Guvnors 'lingered unobtrusively at railway stations to identify rival supporters to be battered in an operation of military-style efficiency. The teenage "scouts" pretended to read timetables or newspapers and did not contact each other as they kept watch. Their reconnaissance was crucial to the Guvnors' campaign of violence because fans from other cities often did not wear team colours and had to be picked out by their accents.'

For good measure, the prosecutor also said we had threatened the former United star Paddy Crerand at his pub in Altrincham. The boozer had been wrecked by a mob of City one night.

It was put over as though we were a huge, highly-organised army with everyone doing exactly as they were directed. All the stuff they raked up about us having generals and lieutenants and intelligence units was a load of bollocks. You just go to the match with your boys and if it kicks, it kicks. Rarely is anyone badly hurt.

The jury watched a film made by a police cameraman of two Leeds fans being attacked outside Maine Road. After a bit more of this treatment, four of the remaining five saw the writing on the wall and changed their pleas to guilty. Ian Valentine stayed not guilty and had all the charges dropped. Maybe we should have all done that – who knows? Many of the other hooligan cases around that time fell apart. Maybe ours would have too, but a lot of us, including myself, were frightened off by looking at seven or eight years in prison. Plus I was bang to rights on camera, there was no escaping that. The four new guilty pleas were adjourned to join the rest of us for sentence until June 5, pending social inquiry reports.

The day of reckoning finally arrives. David Sumner reprises the case. He lays it on with a trowel. He even says that one of the undercover detectives was so stressed out by the fear that he might be caught that he had a breakdown during the operation. He also reads some choice extracts from Vincent George's 'War Games' diary. We all sit there in a row and I'm thinking, who the fuck is this kid Vincent George? I had never met him in my life but his little book of cuttings was helping the police to put us away.

Then it's Judge Clark's turn. I'm first up for sentencing. He goes into one about how I have tarnished the good name of English sport and how people like myself, who enjoy Saturday afternoon recreational violence, have to be stopped. He says he has no alternative but to impose custodial sentence.

And then he says, 'I sentence you to twenty-one months in prison. You are banned from attending a match at any British football ground for a period of ten years,'

Twenty-one months! What a result. After all that. I thought, I'm out in twelve, maximum. My family in court were upset but I was relieved. It had been a traumatic period and now at least I knew what I was getting. I could go to jail and get on with it.

The dock officer takes me down. He says, 'We had a bet downstairs that you were getting six or seven years.'

They put me in the cage but by now I don't care. The screws are amazed at the sentence. One says, 'I'm not lying, mate, you got a right result there.'

They start to bring the rest of the lads down, one by one. Chris is next.

'Eighteen months.' he says.

Then the others.

'Fifteen months.'

'A year.'

'Six months.'

Twelve of us were done that day. Seven went to jail, one went to a young offenders' institution and four of the younger lads, including Rodney, Adrian Gunning and Jamie Roberts, got community service.

The cops were praised by the judge and afterwards went round mouthing off all over the media about how marvellous they were. Nineteen people pleading guilty to affray and riot and violent disorder was a success for them. They were heroes because they had secured convictions while a lot of similar cases were crashing. It made them look great. The main officer who ran the unit, Malcolm George, is now the national police expert on football hooliganism. Shortly afterwards, it was announced that the team that formed the nucleus of the investigations would be going to the World Cup in Italy in 1990 to keep watch on hooligans.

But the way the prison system worked then, you only served half of your sentence. With the time I had served on remand, I would be out on parole in six months. In fact I was out five months later on weekend home leave. If you think of the work that was involved in that case, six month's intelligence, lots of police expenditure, dawn raids on forty houses, sixteen months waiting to be dealt with, it must have cost hundreds of thousands of pounds. And I got twenty-one months. I often wonder if the Old Bill really were as happy with that as they made out.

After the court case, we were taken straight to Walton Prison in Liverpool. The screw were winding us up on the way, giving it loads on the coach, 'They're all Scousers here, mate, they don't like Mancs. You'd better watch yourselves in the showers.'

Actually the inmates were brilliant with us. We got to reception and could hear them saying, 'Are you the Guvnors, are you the Guvnors? The Guvnors are here.' They looked after us well. They knew all about us because the case had been in the national papers and on TV and radio. They gave us all new gear. In those days it was all uniforms, you couldn't wear your own clothes. We got new tee-shirts. You got two pairs of underpants each, a pair of jeans, a pair of black shoes, socks. If they thought you were nothing, you got the shittiest pair of jeans that were too tight and too small for you, you got shoes with no laces in that didn't fit, you got socks full of holes. We got well boxed off. The cons dished them out, trustees, all lads who were near the end of their sentence or just model prisoners. I learned that in jail you are all in the same boat and a lot of the Manc versus Scouser stuff goes out of the window. Everyone helps each other out.

We were sent to our cells. Chris was put on a different wing and so I was on my own. I was led to my cell, opened the door and the screw said, 'Welcome to your new home.'

He pushed me in and shut the door. There was nothing in the room but porno pictures and a scruffy bed. Here we go. Stuck in this hole. The first thing I intended doing was cleaning the place up.

I was sharing with someone else. There were footsteps

outside and I heard one Scouser say to another, 'Here y'are mate, there's a fucking nigger in your cell.'

I looked up and saw someone peering through the window, this kid with long hair. I thought, I've got a right cunt here. But he came in the cell and he turned out to be all right. We got on well.

The next day, we had a chance to read the headlines:

## GUVNORS BANNED FOR 75 YEARS (*Daily Mirror*)

## JAILED THUGS GIVEN TEN-YEAR BAN FROM SOCCER! (*The Sun*)

### 'Governors' jailed as police infiltrate football gang (*Daily Telegraph*)

### Guvnors' boss jailed (*Manchester Evening News*)

There were nice mugshots of me looking a right hood. Later that day, Pat Berry got fifteen months, on top of a twenty-one month stretch he was already serving, for 'leading a gang of up to thirty hooligans which roamed the city centre hunting Aston Villa supporters after a match at Maine Road.' Dave Goodall received a suspended sentence and a £1,000 fine. Others got community service and everyone was banned from football for various periods. Chapman, who was twenty-seven, got a £500 fine. He had confessed in his witness statement. All the lads done were from Greater Manchester, which shows how tight-knit our firm was. No outsiders.

Many got community service because the judge said that hooliganism was a community offence and so they should pay the public back. Of the whole sentencing, they gave out about twenty years, between twenty of us. I know a lad from Man United who was on a ferry when it kicked off with West Ham and he got seven years for robbing jewellery off the boat, because it was football-related. He wasn't even a hooligan, he'd just gone for a snatch. That puts it in perspective. One way I did suffer, though, was when the *Manchester Evening News* revealed that I had worked as a stripper at ladies' parties, under the name Mickey Hot Rocks. I got ribbed for that something terrible.

It turned out there were a lot of Mancs in Walton, some of whom I knew, like Steve Bryan, who I later went into business with. I had no trouble in there at all, partly because we had a little clique and partly because of me being a big lad and the way I carry myself. If you are weak and you look weak, you can get murdered. There weren't that many smackheads in jail then either; they cause a lot of mither inside, always pestering people. I suppose the good news was that the week after we were sent down, City were promoted, finishing second in Division Two. Another big day I missed out on.

Jail is not as hard as it could be if you can get the things you want. If you have a strong character and put yourself about, you can get pretty much anything in jail. You can get milk, decent meat, all the good stuff. You don't have to get the shit. You can bag yourself a decent job. It can be harder for your family and friends; they think you are suffering in jail when really you are getting plenty of sleep, using the gym twice a day, reading, having a break. What more do you want? If you like going to the gym and eating, it is the best way to put on weight and get yourself fit. I came out fit as fuck, like a raging bull. Of course it has its downside, you can't see your family.

I was in Walton for about twelve weeks and then moved to Wymott, a semi-open prison in Leyland, Lancashire, where I shared with Chris until we both got our own cells, next door to each other. It was like going back to school. Each block is a 'T' shape, with an A house, B house and C house. I was on B house. It had fourteen cells, you were allowed your own door-key and could have a stereo in your room and your own television which you could watch until 8pm. They would just lock the main wing door and we could have all the cells open, twenty-odd men running wild, smuggling in dope for draw parties, everyone saving their biscuits and cakes from visits until Friday night, taking your shirts off, covering the lights to make the room go blue, playing music dead loud and having a rave right there on the wing. It was wild.

One night we were in there and everyone was on the smoke. I got a bit dizzy after a few puffs because I don't smoke. They knew I'd do anything for a laugh, so one lad took a broomstick and said, 'Bet you can't do this, Mickey. Get the brush, look at the light, walk round it, put it on the floor, jump over it three times and run down the corridor.'

So I get this brush, go round and round, jump over it, lose my bearings totally, hit every fucking wall, smash my head open, pouring blood, and collapse on the floor. I pretend I have done myself in proper. I'm lying there and they all rush round me going, 'Fuckin' hell, he's done in.'

'I think he's dead.'

Just as they were about to call the screws, I went, 'Yaaargh' and jumped up and they ran for their lives.

Wymott was full of Mancs. There were a few queers about as well, although I think the gang rapes that you hear about in America are very rare over here. Some strange things do go on though and I think the officers are aware of it and just let it happen. On that wing, the screws knew that Chris and I were pretty game and if they looked like losing control they would sometimes say to us, 'Will you sort it out for us?'

We would get extra privileges for keeping things sweet. If someone was playing up, being a cunt and ruining things for everyone else, they'd say, 'If you weigh him in, Mike, don't weigh him in too badly. He needs a smacking.'

They can't do it themselves because they'd get sacked, so what they try to do is manipulate you. You have to be careful you aren't used. You can't do everything they say, give someone a slap just because they don't like him. The thing is, they know what everyone is in for and it always comes out in the end. People who are in for molesting kids and that sort of stuff, and aren't put on rule forty-two, get weighed in and deserve it. Most prisons have their own little groups that run wings but they are hard places to control because, once you get your feet too well in, you get moved out very quickly.

Our jailing was not the end of the firm's woes. Not long after our sentencing, eight lads pleaded guilty at Oldham Crown Court to their involvement in the Battle of Piccadilly in February, 1988. They had arrested seventeen altogether, but the charges were dropped against half of them. The court was told that seventy to eighty City boys met in the early evening in the Lower Turks pub in Shudehill, where the landlord overheard them talking about attacking the Manchester United football special train that was due back from Arsenal. Then they went to Nicklebys, near Piccadilly Station, avoiding London Road so the police wouldn't spot them. Eventually they moved on the station and sent in what the prosecutor called a 'skirmish party' of between ten and twenty-five lads while the rest waited at the bottom of the approach, under an archway. When the scouts walked onto the platform, there were only a few United around.

According to the report in the *Oldham Chronicle*:

A police officer ushered the City fans back, an effort which met with very little resistance. Outside the station, PC Duffy was joined by two other police officers, who attempted to usher them down the approach.

Mr Wright [prosecuting] said that civilian observers got the impression that the police officers were being lured away from the station.

One of the officers, PC Martin, was hit on the nose after an order to stand and turn was given to the mob. PC Duffy ran past and attempted, by using his truncheon, to create a safe distance between the group and the arrest.

The officers were encircled by the mob, who initially attempted to free the prisoner and then attacked the police officers.

Mr Wright said that PC Duffy tried to fend them off with a truncheon in one hand and his helmet in the other.

Duffy was then hit on the head with a hammer, fracturing his skull. He later spent eight months off work. A lad called David Clayton, from Oldham, was sent to a young offenders' institution for three years for using the hammer.

# 14
## *The Doors*

When I came out of prison, I took a change of direction. I had to stay away from the football. Despite all of the trials and arrests, plenty of City boys hadn't been caught and were still at it. Even before the start of the 1989–90 season, it had kicked off at Bolton at a game between City and Wanderers for Nat Lofthouse's testimonial. There were fights on the terraces, running battles between fans and ten arrests inside the ground. Chief Inspector David Russell of Bolton Police said, 'It's obvious some people still go to matches intent on causing trouble.' Well spotted.

That was followed swiftly by the massive kick-off with United at Maine Road in September (see Chapter Four). It was the first time we had played them in the League for two-and-a-half years and they were well up for it. They somehow got hold of 200 tickets for the North Stand and also had firms in other City sections of the ground. In February, 1990, there was even worse violence in the city centre after we drew with United at Old Trafford. This report was from the *Daily Mail*:

*A man was critically ill last night after more than 200 hooligans rampaged through a city. The victim was on a life support machine after surgery for head, face and chest injuries.*

*The mob of Manchester United supporters caused thou-*

sands of pounds damage as they charged from pub to pub after their drawn derby match with Manchester City.

'It was absolute Wild West-style madness,' said the land-lady at the worst-hit pub, the Crown and Kettle, a listed building in central Manchester. Police estimated the damage there at £30,000, but the management put the figure far higher. Doormen had barricaded the entrances as they saw the mob approaching, but they forced their way in.

'They hurled broken furniture through every one of our fourteen Victorian glass windows,' said the landlady, who asked not to be named. 'There were eighty people inside, mainly women. We were all on the floor hiding under tables and behind the bar, screaming as broken glass showered down. It lasted for seven minutes and it was sheer terror.

'The woman disc jockey and her girl assistant were both cut and taken to hospital. One needed stitches to her arm, the other suffered a badly gashed leg. We were shouting out, "It's only women in here, please leave us", but it made no difference. I lay on top of my eighteen-year-old daughter to try to protect her.'

At the Land o' Cakes pub in Great Ancoats Street, a passing youth was knocked to the floor by a thug bran-dishing a table leg. He was treated in hospital

Landlord Norman Molloy was hit in the groin by another table leg as he tried to bar the door to his pub. Windows were smashed by a volley of missiles.

Mr Molloy said, 'It was a crazed rampage. Police with dogs turned up, and bottles and pint pots were flying. There was little the police could do against such numbers.'

Police said there were twenty separate incidents and nine people were arrested.

The guy who was badly hurt, Gerard Connor, was one of a group of United fans attacked with bar stools and pool cues late that evening in Wetherbys night club. He was on a life support machine for a while and suffered partial brain damage. In a phone call to a newspaper, the Beer Monsters claimed credit for orchestrating the violence. The caller claimed many of the City gang were Protestant and belonged to the Orange Lodge, while United sided with Catholics. He added, 'Fighting is one thing but it is getting out of hand.'

I had to get away from that shit. I devoted my energies to more positive things. I had been with Altitude Scaffolding until they were bought out by a South African firm called Cape, a massive organisation. Then I went working on the mainland oil refinery at Stanlow, Ellesmere Port. I had been there five or six years and was a shop steward when I was jailed. They picked me up in Manchester every morning by minibus and I was earning good money. I moved to Prestwich and got a nice house and a mortgage. I kept the football very secret from my employers. In the day time I was a proper, normal hardworking guy, up in the morning to take the dog for a walk, 'Morning, Mrs Jones,' then working nine to five, behaving myself. In fact, my neighbours were gobsmacked when I was arrested. They thought I was such a nice lad. But at weekends I turned into a maniac.

When I came out of jail, I had been blacklisted from the shop stewards' list and couldn't get back on the site. I went to work for this bloke as a labourer, for £20 a day in my hand, scaffolding. I had been taking home £350 for a five-day week as a shop steward; £500 if I worked weekends. So I was pissed off. Knowing about the scaffolding game, I decided to go it on my own. I advertised for someone to help me and said to the guy I was working for, 'Really, you can't pay me enough. I've got a mortgage. You are paying me £120 a week, it's just not enough.'

We didn't fall out, I just went my way and he got someone else. He even gave me a subbing job to help get me started, so I brought some of my own lads in. I did a bit more subbing, started to get a bit of gear together, 'acquiring' a bit here and there, buying a bit, then I got a wagon and went from there. It was long hours but then I wasn't devoting all my spare time to football any more. I did, however, have another occupation that presented almost as many opportunities for violence.

\* \* \*

Since the age of twenty-one, I had worked as a night club bouncer. Donald did a bit of door work, knew a few guys in the game and found me my first job at a club called Fagins, on Oxford Road. It faced another well-known club, Rotters, which is now a McDonalds. They paid me £12 a night. It was rough. Rotters often had stag nights from rough-arse places like Liverpool, St Helens, Widnes and Wigan coming over, coachloads of out-of-town firms. Some of them would come into Fagins and after a few beers you would be fighting all night for your poxy £12. All the Manchester lads went to a place called Pips, on Fennel Street, which later became the Konspiracy and was shut down by the police. It was a bit of a City hangout. At 2am, the boys would make their way to Rotters to kick fuck out of the lads getting on the coach trips. There would be mass battles,

Manchester versus whoever. We would stand in the doorway and watch it all.

Fagins had about ten doormen. There was no formal training. Recruitment was a case of someone saying, 'My mate's a bit of a hard lad, put him on the door.' If you could look after yourself, you got the job. They didn't expect you to be a boxer or a martial artist as long as you were a bit tasty and streetwise. You had to have a bit of diplomacy but there were no exams to take. Mike Fo, the head doorman, was a martial arts guy. He has his own firm now called Protech Security. He gave me the job, working the door every Thursday, Friday and Saturday. It was very regimented. You had to stand at a pillar, then move round to the next pillar, like a rota, keeping your eye on things. That was how the management wanted it. The manager was a little fellow called Paul, he looked like Tattoo out of *Love Boat*.

It was a disco-cabaret club. You would get bands like Showaddywaddy and The Real Thing, all the has-beens that were on their arses and had to play poxy clubs for a few quid. The uniform was white shirts, black jackets and dicky bows. The head doorman wore a white jacket, which usually ended up covered in blood. In those days you could hit someone on the nose and there would be no comebacks. Nine times out of ten they were outsiders anyway and were pissed up and out of order. These days you have to be more careful who you hit; too many comebacks.

I had been there a fortnight when I knocked someone out. A coach party was in from out of town and started fighting. With my terrace background, I was used to fighting one way: get the boys together and steam in. I assumed the ten lads on the door would do the same.

I shouted, 'Come me on, all together, let's have 'em, let's rush them.'

Mike Fo shook his head in despair. 'You can't do that, Mickey. It's not a football match.'

We made our way over the trouble spot and tried to split it up. One of these kids came at me so I banged him one and he fell over. I bent over him on the floor to drag him up and throw him out and he punched me on the nose. I gave him a real crack. Unfortunately, it left him in a bit of a bad way and everyone in the club had seen me hit him. Someone called an ambulance and the stretcher crew came in. I took my jacket off in a pathetic attempt at disguise, ran downstairs and hid.

I waited a while, then I ventured up to the entrance see if the coast was clear. The guys' mates were still in the club, saw me and rushed the doorway, yelling, 'That's him, the black bastard there, he thinks he's hard, let's 'ave him.' Fortunately the rest of the doormen weighed in and and we threw them out. After that I was told, in no uncertain terms, 'You can't do that sort of thing.'

'Yeah, fair enough.'

We had a code to signal trouble. The DJ or the bar staff would say over a microphone, 'Mr Stans to the dance floor,' or, 'Mr Stans to the top bar.' That meant there was a fight there. I called it all the time on purpose, pressed the panic buzzers, just to wind the lads up. You'd hear them shouting, 'It's kicking off in the doorway!' and they'd come charging through, half a ton of beef, knocking punters over, only to get there and find nothing. Their response was to tell me, 'One of these days you'll do it, none of us will take any notice, and you'll get hammered.'

One night we were standing at the cloakroom at closing time. The customers were getting their coats and we were being polite, saying, 'Goodnight mate, goodnight miss.'

This lad said, 'Goodnight mate.' He walked down the steps, turned back, smacked me right on the jaw and knocked me unconscious down the stairs. The other doormen chased after him while I was trampled by the queue of customers pushing out. I lost my shoe, had a black eye and a swollen mouth and the lad got away. To this day I don't know who he was.

Then there was the night when we had one of the those massive, lone-wolf maniacs who nobody wants to deal with. This guy was a well-known heavy, about six feet four and built like a bear. He had been barred from the club but turned up this night and the lads on the door were too frightened to stop him coming in. They sent me to tell him he was barred. They had three steps in the middle of the club, near the stage, and this bloke was so big that when I was standing on the top step and he was at the bottom, our eyes were just about level.

'Er, listen mate, I'm afraid you're barred from here. I'll have to ask you to leave the club, please.'

He leaned over, confidentially, and growled in my ear, 'Do you want to keep your fucking kneecaps?'

Now that's fighting talk, wherever you come from, but I knew that if I hit him I would need some backup. I tried to front him, saying, 'You're going to have to leave, mate,' but I knew things had gone too far.

I took three quick steps and headbutted him full in the face. Amazingly, he fell backwards onto a table, spraying drinks and glass all over a group of women in their best dresses. I leapt on top of him, punching like a threshing machine, and he blacked out, thank fuck. If he'd hit me, he would have killed me. The other doormen were now brave enough to come over. We picked him up to carry him out but as we passed through the first set of doors, he came round. He saw me and went off his head, rearing up to his full height and roaring like a lion while the lads struggled to hold him. He threatened to shoot me, kill me, cut me into pieces.

I kept a safe distance and said, 'You know where I am, come back any time.'

'I know who you are, you train at the Cavendish gym and you drive such-and-such a car.'

He fucking knew who I was! I thought, it's on top now. But it turned out to be all wind and there were no reprisals, although I was looking over my shoulder for a few weeks. Fortunately, most lads think the next morning, oh well, I got a smack, leave it at that.

Admittedly, I was a headbanger on the door. If anyone fucked about, I would belt them. The other lads would say, 'Get hold of Mike, he'll sort it.'

At that stage, Manchester wasn't the gang-oriented city it became. There were fewer of those people who have reputations and who you have to watch out for, people who are out to make their mark as criminals or 'gangsters.' If there were any around, I was too young to know or care. I'd get the odd threat but you get them all your life. Now I know all the 'heads.' I still think Manchester is a great city. There are lots of good places to go.

I later moved on from Fagins to Applejacks, near the Britannia Hotel. It was an exclusive club then, all white jackets, and that was a good job. All the rich geezers went there and the doormen parked their cars for them.

One bloke gave me the keys to his Range Rover and I fucked off for an hour around town. I saw all my mates working on other doors, shouted them to get in and come for a spin. I came back and the bloke had only been in the club for ten minutes and had been waiting for his car for ages. I was lucky not to get sacked.

The management had a policy that if girls were too ugly, they couldn't come in. They only wanted nice-looking girls in the club. We were supposed to make up excuses to turn them away but we just used to say, 'Sorry love, you're too ugly, fuck off.'

They used to give it right back: 'Who are you calling ugly? Look at the state of you.'

Who gives a damn?

What did bug me was that they didn't want too many black people in. We were actually told, 'We only want about ten to fifteen black guys in, keep the rest of them out.'

The head doorman was my close friend Trevor Dore, who is black, yet he was prepared to implement the policy. I wasn't happy with it. Apart from being half-caste myself, many of my mates and the lads I played football with were black. They would come into town for a night out, all smart, turn up at the club to see their mate Mickey and I was expected to knock them back. I couldn't go along with it and in the end I left.

I worked on other doors all around town and resumed when I came out of prison. The friends I had were still going out on the town at weekends but I cut myself away a bit. The early nineties saw the growth of door security companies; instead of a club employing its own doormen, it would use the services of an agency, which might supply bouncers to many different pubs and clubs.

It was a sensible idea because you really need experts who know the business and, more importantly, know people. You can't just stick Joe Bloggs on the door, no matter how big he is. You need the right people on the right places. If you do a door in Moss Side, you don't stick five white rugby players on the door. They'll get butchered. You get five black guys who know the score.

I saw the way things were going and started a security company with my mate Steve Bryan. Like me, Steve was doing door work, he's intelligent and has good views on things. We named the company Loc-19 Security Limited after the canal lock at the Canal Bar on Whitworth Street, where we did the door, and began supplying doormen to pubs and clubs throughout Greater Manchester. Between us, we knew a lot of good lads.

It's high-profile work. You're in the spotlight all the time. One day someone will write a book about the Manchester club scene but not me. Too many people wouldn't like the publicity. Guns were becoming commonplace, with the 'drug wars' in Moss Side, kids walking around in body armour, bouncers being butchered at the most famous club, the Hacienda, and so on. We often found ourselves working the doors that nobody else would do, danger spots like The Limit. That was very lively. We had bullets coming through the door. It wasn't unusual for the doormen to wear bulletproof vests and carry CS gas and a tool, because when they had all-nighters, the other clubs would shut at 2am and everyone would pile down to The Limit, and they wanted to come in, no matter what. You knew that some time in the period up to 4am there would be a confrontation, every weekend, and it would be bad. It had your heart racing, thinking, 'Here we go again.'

Fortunately the gangland violence quietened down a lot after 1995, when the four or five main men came together and sorted out a truce. If there is a dispute now, compensation is paid to the injured party. It prevents warfare breaking out again. People who don't pay up might have their hand smashed with a hammer or be shot through a kneecap. No-one goes to the police any more. It is a street code. The rash ones are the young lads. Almost all those 'gang' deaths over a period of a few years were kids under twenty-five. They are reckless, there are sixteen-year-old kids that will put a bullet in your head for nothing.

The police make dossiers of incidents at club and if things are too hot they'll oppose the licence when the manager re-applies. There was one particularly bad episode at The Limit which they learned about and the club was closed. But we had plenty of other doors and by now I had also set up a firm called MKM Scaffolding. I built it up and was employing, on and off, six to eight people. It was enough to earn me a good living.

Once again, however, jail fucked me up. My second sentence was for self-defence, as far as I am concerned. I may have gone over the top but if someone's gunning for you and you can resolve it there and then, you do. The Canal Bar is a big, popular pub with a DJ, next to the Hacienda. On this particular night, I was driving from door to door paying the wages to the lads. I received a call on my radio saying there was a disturbance. I drove to the Canal Bar and found our Chris, who was working for us, and the other doormen discussing what had happened. Some young lads had apparently turned up and threatened them with a handgun.

Five minutes later, a white car drove past with two

white kids and two black kids in it. One of them flashed what looked like a gun at the doorway. People came running into the club, ducking, yelling, 'There's someone out there with a gun.'

The car drove a little further on until it stopped in a queue of traffic at the lights outside the Hacienda. I said to the doormen, 'Let's fucking have 'em.'

Looking back, it was a daft thing to do. They could have blown my head off. But the adrenalin was pumping. We swamped the car, climbing on it, pulling bits off. Two of them got out and legged it but we dragged out the other two, beat the crap out of them in the middle of the road and smashed every window and light in the car. No decorum, those lads were damaged.

A voice said, 'Mickey Francis, you're under arrest.'

Uh-oh. Where the fuck did they come from?

I ignored it and began to walk back to the Canal Bar. A policeman came behind me.

'Mickey Francis, you're under arrest for grievous bodily harm and criminal damage.'

'Fuck off, you don't know the full story, let me tell you what happened.'

I was still walking, thinking on my feet. How do I get out of this? We reached the Canal Bar and the copper suddenly gripped me by the collar, which was a mistake, as the bar was full of lads who knew me. Someone chinned the copper. Still he wouldn't let go. Someone else grabbed another copper in a headlock. I could have escaped but I decided not to run. Once I could explain things, they'd realise it was self-defence.

To cut a long story short, the police sent for loads of reinforcements and there was a big battle. I was nicked with two others and taken to Bootle Street. One copper had a slight bruise to his hand, a bit of a bruise on his face, nothing too bad. They charged me with affray.

When it was put in court, the judge looked at me and said, 'I have seen your past history, Mr Francis, and you seem to like being in control of men. This situation could have been resolved in a different way.'

Which it could have been. I could have left it and let them get away.

The prosecutor had said, 'When you arrived at the club, you took it upon yourself to dish out your own discipline, didn't you?'

He was right. But I pleaded not guilty and had the trial, over two days, although I was caught bang to rights by two police officers who, unbeknown to me, had been parked across the street and had witnessed the entire incident. The kids were seventeen-year-old nobodies and, to make things worse, no gun was ever found; they did find a piece of pipe cut to look like a gun. I couldn't even go and get revenge because they were kids. The jury found me guilty and I was jailed for twelve months in 1995.

I was sent back to Strangeways again. A few guys who worked for us on the doors were in there for various things. I asked the officer on induction to be put on G wing, where my mates were. Two hours later, I was where I wanted to be, in my own cell with a telly. I got talking to a lad who worked the door at the Hacienda, he was doing four years for breaking someone's jaw, and he said he was working on the food servery.

'I wouldn't mind a job there.'

'There's no room at the moment,' he said.

I went down at tea-time and just put a white jacket on.

'What are you doing?' the screw said.

'I'm on the servery.'

'Who said?'

'I said.'

'You're not supposed to.'

'I'll just work here for nothing until there's a space.'

'All right, fair enough.'

I worked on the servery, never got paid for two weeks until someone moved out and then I took their place officially. I had it boxed off, as much food as I wanted, my own room, from day one. It was like a holiday camp. What also helped, strangely enough, was a two-page article in the *Manchester Evening News*, headlined 'The Twilight Zone,' about conflict between different groups on the club doors in Manchester. My name and picture were all over it. After that, some people looked at me differently, although I wasn't out to play the big cheese. Inmates talk all the time and the screws know who you are. Maybe they worry that they are going to get jumped on the way home, even though I would never do that.

I think the days are over where people in prison want to be the 'daddy,' where they say, 'I'll take him out and I'll get his fucking perch.' People are more frightened now of what could happen in reprisals if they try to do something to you. I have upset people in my past but not enough, I don't think, that someone would want to kill me. A lot of people wanted to know me to big themselves up, make them feel like they are something in jail. The Strangeways screws respect you if you have a bit of a name in Manchester. Once you go to a jail outside the city, then you're just another number.

I was getting a bit irritated. I kept getting told I was going to be moved out of the jail to somewhere else and

I didn't want to go because Strangeways was handy for my visits, the phonecard lasted longer and the television was a great help in jail when we were banged up at 8pm. Also, I got all the idiots on my case, like smackheads. They don't stop mithering you for stuff. Seven years ago there weren't as many drug addicts in jail. Now there are loads. They can get anything they want in jail; they can get more drugs inside than they can when they're out. I started knocking them all out.

It began one morning when I lost my temper with some cunt in the phone box, dragged him into the recess and banged him out. Then some Scouse kid threatened me while having a shave one morning because I had pushed a trolley over his foot. I went in his cell and battered him. The screws knew I was doing it and just turned a blind eye. The last straw was this kid at breakfast one day. I served him some bacon.

He says, 'What the fucking hell is that?'

'That's all you get mate, one rasher.'

It was a proper sad ration, believe me. It was nearly all fat with just a tiny bit of bacon.

He says, 'I'm not having that,' and lobbed it in my face.

I was so taken aback that I just stood there with my mouth open while the kid walked off.

A screw had been watching. He said to me, 'You're not going to let that go, are you, Francis?'

'Am I fuck.'

I'm still wearing a green pinny and rubber gloves but I stalk round the wings, all the cells, every door, trying to find this cunt, going mad now, thinking I'm going to kill him.

In the meantime, someone has told this lad, 'That was

Mickey Francis. You had better go and apologise or he'll do you in.'

He comes downstairs into the kitchen recess. I'm washing the pots, still fuming.

'I just want to apologise to you, mate.'

'Come in here and apologise then.'

He comes in. I smack him on the jaw, he hits the window, smashes it and does his nose in. The screws having their breakfast have seen me and just shut the door. So I filled him in and walked out. His nose was a mess. One of the screws called Crickson, he didn't like me anyway, went straight off the wing to reception and had me kicked off the jail. I went back to my pots and a screw came up and said, 'Francis, you had better leave that, you're getting moved tomorrow.'

I went to Risley, near Warrington. It was like going back fifty years. There were holding cells on the bottom floor with no glass in them, just wire mesh, no toilet, no soap, no money and it was freezing. They had a thing called cell association which meant you could go out of your cell but you had to go into someone else's. It was horrible. Then I got a job in the wash house, which wasn't too bad. I was there for six months and that was long enough.

* * *

In November, 1990, thirty-one United fans were arrested at their homes after a fifteen-month investigation by the Omega squad. Operation Mars was supposed to break United's firm. Things went better for them than they had for us, however. The police were refused permission to give their evidence from behind screens and charges of conspiracy were dropped. Finally, in July, 1993, charges against nineteen of the alleged hooligans were struck out by a judge who ruled that they had taken too long to come to court.

City lads didn't fare so well. In May, 1991, the trial had begun of lads involved in the incident at Wetherbys in which the bloke had been kicked into a coma. As usual, it was at an out-of-town court, this time Bolton Crown, to prevent witness and jury intimidation. Originally ten City fans were sent to trial but some, including Donald Farrer, had the case dismissed.

The prosecutor described mobs roaming around the streets of Manchester city centre armed with beer glasses, pool cues and snooker balls.

## Thugs pay the price for vicious soccer riot

Two of Manchester City's most violent soccer thugs were behind bars today.

Martin Townsend and Rodney Rhoden, vicious hooligans who wouldn't learn, paid a heavy price for their part in a derby match riot which left a Reds fan clinging to life.

After a month-long trial at Bolton Crown Court, twenty-eight-year-old Townsend was jailed for four years and Rhoden, eighteen, was sent to a young offenders' institution for two years. Both have a string of violence convictions and were rounded up by police in 1989 in their Operation Omega probe into the feared Guvnors and Young Guvnors gangs.

Rhoden and Townsend were banned from attending matches – Townsend for seven years and Rhoden for five. But Townsend could not keep away and travelled to Italy for the World Cup, only to be booted out by the authorities.

Four other City fans were also jailed for taking part in the riot in February last year by Judge John Townsend at Bolton. An attack on Wetherby's night club by a group of up to sixty Blues fans was 'a serious crime against the peace of Manchester,' the judge said.

Townsend and another lad got four years each, Rodney got two years and several others were jailed.

City were reported to the FA following an incident at a home game against Oldham in September, 1991, when the referee Peter Willis was hit with a hot meat pie. A year later, City and Spurs yobs slugged it out behind the Kippax. In May, 1993, 200 fans invaded the pitch during the FA Cup quarter-final against Tottenham and the Spurs goalie Eric Thorsvedt was booted up the backside by a father of four. Thirty-seven lads were arrested and the club was fined £50,000 and ordered to close the ground for one match. In October the same year, Donald Farrer was in the papers again after slipping into Holland for the European Championships with a passport in the name of Mike Tyson. He told a reporter that he had also used a passport in the name Freddy Krueger, the character in Nightmare on Elm Street. In May, 1993, a troop of Everton launched an assault on the Dry Bar in Oldham Street after the last game of the season. And in 1995, there was heavy fighting when Man United infiltrated the Main Stand and the Umbro Stand at Maine Road. Later there were running battles across town.

These and other incidents I read about in the paper,

or heard about from the lads. I was no longer involved. Like Donald, I had become business-minded and was busy earning a living. When I went into prison the second time, I was owed about £40,000 for various scaffolding jobs but had been unable to complete many of them. Bob Green, who had got me into the game, had started his own firm called Crest Scaffolding and he took my work on for me. When I came out, he bought my business, took all my scaffolding, my wagon, everything. I put the money down as a deposit on a yard with lock-up units. I rent them out to small firms and now it turns over a nice income.

The security work continued to expand. We built it up to about eighty lads on the doors at night, with forty on in the daytime at shops, building sites and other premises. I was also developing other interests that involved less hassle. Recently I launched St James Development Capital, which supplies credit reference, brokerage and debt collection. I am involved in some exciting plans to import wine from Italy. I have stepped back a bit from the door work, although I continue to work as a consultant and adviser on close protection and other aspects of security. I'm doing okay and I have big plans. I don't think I've done too badly for a ragamuffin kid from Moss Side.

# *Epilogue*

WILL I ever go back?

My ban from football matches ends in June, 1999. Then I will be free to pay in wherever I please – if Manchester City don't ban me again after reading this book. Football has a powerful pull for many of us. Mark Fiorini, one of the lads who was convicted with me, was recently fined £100 for breaching his ten-year exclusion order. He was spotted by police at a home match. He said his children had pestered him to take them to a game.

I know that if I returned to the terraces, I could raise 100–200 lads in no time. I hear that City get battered these days. They've no mob. To re-build the firm and put them back on the map would be a top buzz – but I'd never do it.

Times change. I came from the days when you could battle all day long without a policeman coming near you, without so much as a, 'Leave it out lads and fuck off.' I was caught because I couldn't walk away. Donald got out but I couldn't stop. If I was going today, I would still feel the pull of the old excitement, the thrill of a fight. Chris is the same. Both of us loved that boost, the power of people asking, 'Where shall we go now, what shall we do now?' That feeling of strength

But you get nicked for swearing now. Coshed and CS-gassed. I'd be a marked man. Once you get a reputation, it's hard to shake it off. In fact, if I was shot in the head tonight and killed, you'd probably read in the papers tomorrow, 'Gangster Shot Dead.' That's how they'd portray me. Yet I'm not a criminal. I don't thieve, I don't rob, I don't deal with drugs. What I have done is have a fight.

People say you are what you make of yourself. That's bollocks. It's your background that makes you. Violence has never bothered me; I grew up with it. I wouldn't flinch if I saw someone getting battered in front of me now. I have seen it a million times. I wouldn't feel any pity for anybody. That's just the way it is.

Looking back, I wouldn't have changed the way we ran the firm, or the way we behaved. I could have been more cautious, more devious, but the police would have caught me sooner or later. I didn't hide. I revelled in it. I knew I was heading for a fall but I couldn't stop.

This is no apology but what I do regret a little are the wasted years, the failure to make something more of myself. I'm doing okay now but I spent years in pursuit of that adrenalin fix, following City all over the country, home and away, chasing all over the shop, in the cold and rain, and at the end of the day I had nothing to show for it but a lengthy charge sheet and a few scars. Now it is all in the past. My last fight at a football match was almost ten years ago and the Mickey Francis you have just read about is not the person you see today.

I'm lucky to be banned from City at the moment. The court did me a favour. They are terrible on the pitch, though the support is fantastic. To go back and start again would be to jeopardise what I have now and that I wouldn't do. I would go to a big game but I'd just watch the match, have a drink and a laugh and go home.

You never know though, do you?